# CONTENTS

THE OPEN UNIVERSITY

Arts/Social Sciences: An Inter-faculty Second Level Course
**Man's Religious Quest**

# Units 9-11
# THE NOBLE PATH OF BUDDHISM

Written by Joseph Masson for the Course Team
and translated by Lawrence Watson and Francis Clark

The Open University Press

The Open University Press
Walton Hall, Milton Keynes
MK7 6AA

First published 1977. Reprinted 1981, 1984

Designed by the Graphic Design Group of the Open University.

Printed in Great Britain by
Speedlith Photo Litho Limited, Stretford, Manchester M32 0JT.

ISBN 0 335 05373 4

For general availability of supporting material referred to in this text, please write to Open University Educational Enterprises Limited, 12 Cofferidge Close, Stony Stratford, Milton Keynes, MK11 1BY, Great Britain.

Further information on Open University courses may be obtained from the Admissions Office, The Open University, P.O. Box 48, Walton Hall, Milton Keynes, MK7 6AB.

1.3

# 1 THE THREE JEWELS

## 1.1 The treasury of Buddhism

When a Buddhist monk is admitted fully into monastic life he performs a ceremony which has as its essential point the threefold repetition of the following triple formula:

*Buddham saranam gacchāmi*—I take the Buddha as my refuge.
*Dhammam saranam gacchāmi*—I take the Dhamma as my refuge.
*Sangham saranam gacchāmi*—I take the Sangha as my refuge.

The Founder, the Law or Doctrine, the Community or Assembly, these are the three refuges of the true Buddhist. According to another classical expression they are the Three Jewels which together form the treasury of Buddhism. A consideration of these three realities is perhaps the best introduction to Buddhism.

*Figure 1 Monk at Bodh Gaya, Bihar, India. (Government of India Tourist Office.)*

## 1.2 The Buddha

The word 'Buddha' which means awakened, illuminated, enlightened, endowed with true wisdom (*Bodhi*), is a title which the Founder of Buddhism obtained only at the time of his supreme spiritual experience.[1] But thirty years had preceded this event and we must say something about the background to the Founder's life during those earlier years.

### 1.2.1 The background

#### 1.2.1.1 Exercise

For a preliminary exercise, it may help you to try to recall and summarize for yourself some salient facts about the religious and social background of ancient India, which provided the environment for the life and work of the Buddha. To refresh your memory refer back to Units 6–7 to *Ling*, §§1.3, 1.5 and 2.30, and to *Encyclopedia*, p. 267.

PLEASE PAUSE HERE

DO NOT READ ON UNTIL YOU HAVE COMPLETED THE EXERCISE

#### 1.2.1.2 Specimen answer

In that period India was populated by peoples who had settled there in very ancient times but who had been subsequently conquered by invading Aryans about 1000 BC. These pastoral peoples had made their way into India in successive waves through the mountain passes of the North-West. You have already studied these developments in the units on Hinduism. As you have seen, the religious treasury of the Aryans was the *Veda* (See *Encyclopedia*, pp. 218–219). In general terms the word Veda signifies sacred knowledge and the object of sacred knowledge; it embraces hymns to the gods, sacrificial formulas, magic formulas, liturgical ordinances and (these were more recent developments) the speculative, philosophical and mystical texts known as the *Upanishads*. The Upanishads are evidence of a desire for spiritual reflection and experience freed from impersonal ritual practices. They heralded a period of free enquiry in which many original thinkers would seek new religious ways; the Buddha was to be one of the greatest of these.

1.2.1.3 From a *social* point of view the Ayran invaders maintained to a considerable extent their racial purity and dominated the indigenous inhabitants. They were divided into two classes, the *brāhmaṇs* who held religious power and were responsible for administering the rites, and the nobles or regional chieftains (*kshatriya*) who held political power and were responsible for government (see *Ling*, §2.30).

1.2.1.4 From an *economic* point of view the nobles who had previously been the chieftains of pastoral peoples in Central Asia now, in India, became

---

[1] It will be useful to refer to parallel passages in your set books, and in the course Reader, as you work through these units. Many of these cross-references will be indicated in the unit text. Here, for example, you could read pages 269–273 of the article by I. B. Horner, 'Buddhism: the Theravada' in Zaehner, R. C. (ed) (1971) *The Concise Encyclopedia of Living Faiths* (2nd edn) Hutchinson, London (hereafter cited as *Encyclopedia*, and §§2.30–2.38 in Ling, T. (1974) *A History of Religion East and West*, Macmillan, London (hereafter cited as *Ling*). The course reader is Foy, W. (ed.) (1977) *Man's Religious Quest: A Reader*, Croom-Helm, London (hereafter cited as *Reader*).

landowners. They were organized according to a feudal system based on alliances and the likelihood of occasional wars. This general situation is clearly reflected in an ancient legislative text:

> To the Brāhmaṇs the Lord entrusts the teaching and the study of the Veda, sacrifices on behalf of themselves and of others, the giving and receiving of gift-offerings. To warriors is entrusted the protection of the people. They too are required to study and make gift-offerings and sacrifices. Farmers are required to rear cattle, to make gifts, to sacrifice and to study, to engage in commerce, to lend money and to cultivate the soil. Finally, the *sūdra* are required to serve the other three classes.

1.2.1.5 The lands of the Buddha's family (whom late texts represent as royal and who seem, at any rate, to have been rich and powerful) were located in North-East India, at the foot of the Himalayas, in Terai. At this time it was a fertile region where cultivated land alternated with forest. The forests were frequented by those engaged in the quest for spiritual enlightenment, seeking solitude for their meditation. The future Buddha would himself one day enter them (see *Encyclopedia*, p. 269f).

*Figure 2  The Renunciation (from Takht-i-Bahi). (Mansell Collection.)*

*Figure 3  The starving Buddha before Enlightenment (probably from Jamal-Garhi). (Mansell Collection.)*

*Figure 4 The Enlightenment
(Gandhara). (Mansell Collection.)*

*Figure 5 The Parinirvana, or
Death of Buddha (from Takt-i-
Bahi). (Mansell Collection.)*

1.2.1.6 The religious complexion of this region was one of great diversity.
Ritualistic brahmanism found itself confronted by a multiplicity of regional
cults having their roots in animism and magic as well as the whole ascetic
and mystical movement in which the future Buddha was to take part. This
latter tendency was based on the clear conviction of the precariousness of all
things, on a belief in endless reincarnations and, therefore, on a desire for
mysterious liberation. This was to be attained through a system of ascetic
and spiritual discipline (yoga) which had originated thousands of years
before.

1.2.1.7 Nothing of indisputable historical fact is known concerning either the
upbringing or the events of the life of the young Siddhārtha (the name of the
future Buddha). The date of his birth is disputed, but it was about 563 BC. It
is possible to affirm that he belonged to the class of the kshatriyas, to the
Sakya clan, and to the family Gautama. In the kind of environment
described above, his youth would have been spent in the comfort and
pleasures normal for someone of his status. There are very frequent references
in the texts to the affluent circumstances of his earlier life. In accordance
with custom he married at the age of sixteen. He had a son Rāhula, the only
child he is known to have had (see *Encyclopedia*, p. 269).

9

## 1.2.2 The crisis

It was when he was twenty-nine years old that Siddhārtha underwent his 'spiritual crisis'. He left behind his family, his property, his privileged class, and became a wondering 'holy man' dressed in rags.

Now read the first extract in the section devoted to Buddhism in the Reader—'The Great Retirement' *(Reader,* §3.1.1)—which gives a dramatic account of his disillusionment with worldly pleasures.

1.2.2.1 The shock which transformed him was a sudden and disturbing awareness of the precariousness of human existence summed up in the drama of old age, illness and death—the three events which illustrate most clearly and brutally this impermanence and uncertainty.

### 1.2.2.2 Exercise

Now read 'The Benares sermon' *(Reader,* §3.1.4) on the nature of suffering; in this text the famous 'Noble Eightfold Path' is marked out. From your reading of this passage, and also of the text of *Reader,* §3.1.1 now write a brief statement of what the Buddha saw as the starting point from which his message of liberation must begin. What is the universal feature of human life on which Buddhism is based? What did the Buddha see as the main characteristics of life in this world?

### PLEASE PAUSE HERE
#### DO NOT READ ON UNTIL YOU HAVE COMPLETED THE EXERCISE

### 1.2.2.3 Specimen answer

Buddhism is based upon an acute awareness of suffering. Certainly this is an awareness which we find generally in the Indian religious tradition, as also an understanding of life as an inescapable round of suffering. But whereas in the Hindu tradition, with all its diversity, we do find other perspectives, the understanding of life as suffering is central to Buddhism, and the way of liberation which the Buddha taught proceeds quite logically from it, as we shall see. The three major characteristics of human life, according to the teaching of the Buddha, are; *dukkha*, suffering; *anicca*, impermanence, and *anatta*, the absence of a permanent enduring, personal identity or 'soul' (see below, §2.5.2).

---

1.2.2.4 The spiritual search which Siddhārtha undertook led him, first of all, to two masters of yoga who were unable to satisfy him. He then decided to make his 'great effort' by himself. For six years, accompanied by five mendicant monks, he practised extreme forms of penitence which endangered his life, but without finding what he sought. Finally he gave them up in favour of more moderate methods. He accepted food, took a bath and sat at the foot of a banyan tree to meditate. From that time onward he followed (as he was to say later) the 'middle way', equidistant from an excess of pleasure (such as that of his youth) and from an excess of penitence (like that of his recent experiments). This quality of 'moderation' is defined in the first paragraph of *Reader,* §3.1.4.

1.2.2.5 It was in this way, by means of a meditative experience, that he attained his enlightenment. (Now read 'The Way to the highest meditations' *(Reader,* §3.4.4) for a systematic description of the Buddhist meditative experience.) The Buddha (and from this time on it is correct to give him this title) was about thirty-five years old. For some weeks he remained immersed in the joy of his 'illumination'. (Now read 'Enjoying the bliss of emancipation', *Reader*, §3.1.2.)

### 1.2.3 The spreading light

1.2.3.1 An urgent question preoccupied the Buddha. Was he, cautiously and jealously, to keep to himself the secret he had discovered, out of fear of losing it, or should he, out of pity, communicate it to others? For they had as much or even more need of instruction and enlightenment than he. After some hesitation he decided to preach. (Now read 'The Buddha hesitates to preach', *Reader*, §3.1.3). He returned to the former companions of his penitence and delivered the Sermon of Benares (see *Encyclopedia*, p. 271; and refer again to the extract from the Sermon in the *Reader*, §3.1.3).

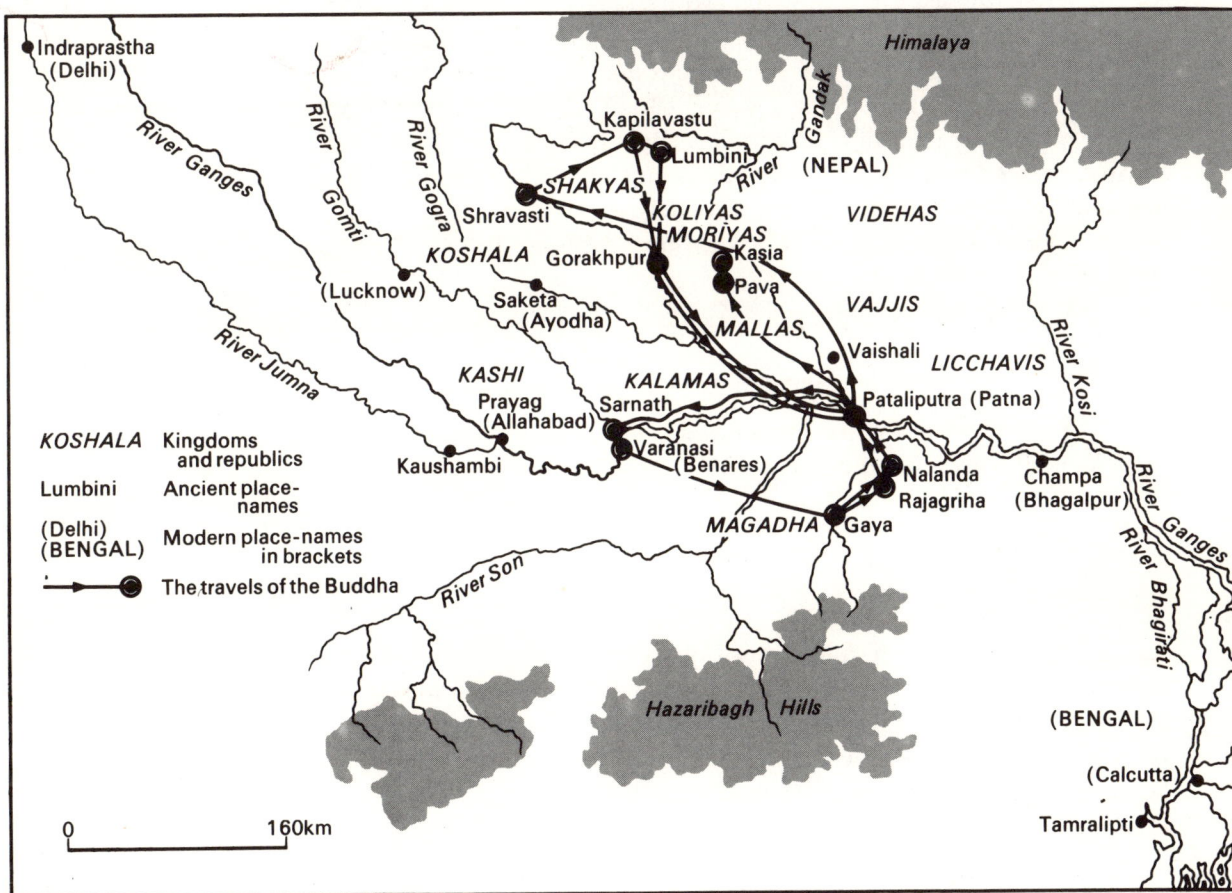

*Figure 6 Map of the travels of the Buddha.*

1.2.3.2 This was the beginning of forty years of itinerant preaching. The Buddha did not escape opposition, notably that stirred up by the ritualistic brāhmans anxious to preserve their religious monopoly. They were annoyed to see an 'uninformed layman', a shaven-headed vagabond, setting himself up as a master of deliverance and, what was more, without recourse to their rituals. On the other hand the Buddha attracted great support from good-hearted young people seeking a solution to the drama of life (see *Reader*, §3.1.6 'Vocation of two friends'). These included nobles who were members of his family or, more generally, of his class: lords and rulers; also a considerable number of brāhmans were won over by his preaching and his replies to questions. In addition there were disciples of humble origin, for Buddhism ignored the barriers of caste: 'It is virtue and not birth which makes a true brāhman'.

1.2.3.3 The grouping of disciples was at first imprecise and inconstant but then became a more identifiable community formed around the master or around the great disciples in a few selected centres where, eventually, important monasteries were established: among them Rajgir, Kapilavastu, Vesalī, Śravastī, Kauśāmbī etc.

1.2.3.4 Except in one or two cases of rejection (notably by one of his cousins) the authority of the Buddha was recognised by all. The later texts of the disciplinary Rule (*Vinaya*, §1.3.3) always appeal (with or without historical basis) to what he has decided. The Buddha is continually consulted and listened to.

### 1.2.4  Death

1.2.4.1 At eighty years of age, weakened by long years of travel and preaching, 'like an old cart that can only be pushed with a great effort' the Buddha fell ill. He gave his last instructions and breathed his last. (Now read 'Last instructions of the Buddha', *Reader*, §3.1.7.) A long account of his passing is given in the Mahāparinibbānasūtra (Sūtra of the Great Final Disappearance); it is certainly carefully arranged but basically factual and has much in common with several other accounts of the same event. After his death and cremation seven towns argued over his ashes before agreeing to share them.

1.2.4.2 Later devotion customarily commemorated the key moments of the Founder's life in four locations:

> In the gounds of Lumbinī, his birth
> At Bodh-Gayā, his enlightenment
> At Benares, his first sermon
> At Kuśinagara, his death

Now read 'The four Holy Places, *Reader*, §3.1.8.

And so the memory of the Buddha was preserved—the memory of an essentially benevolent Master with very practical views, ignoring 'irrelevant' questions in order to prescribe, like a good doctor, the remedy for the pain of the world. For this rejection of theoretical subtleties, see *Reader*, §3.4.5 'Questions which do not help spiritual progress'.

## 1.3   The Doctrine: the Dhamma

### 1.3.1  The word of the Buddha

The word *Dhamma* (*Dharma*), which is used to designate the original doctrine of the Buddha is not exclusively Buddhist but is one of the classical terms of Indian religion. In Hinduism one finds *Manavadharma-śāstra* (the Laws of Manu) and *sanatanadharma* (the eternal, unchanging law or duty which fixes for everyone his nature, his station etc.).

In Buddhism, the term signifies the truth discovered by the Buddha at the time of his enlightenment and subsequently preached by him and by his disciples in the course of their public ministry. It is 'the word of the Buddha', the praises of which are repeatedly sung in the texts. This 'word' is described as 'harmonious of expression, giving delight and pleasure, useful to salvation and true' (Suttanipāta, III, 3). Everything which the Buddha has taught is true (Dīgha-Nikāya, III, 135).

One text summarizes this teaching by presenting it as the discovery of a method for destroying the causes of suffering: 'The Tathāgata (the Buddha), the great monk, has shown the cause and revealed the means of destruction of all elements produced by a cause' (Mahāvagga, 23, 10; refer again to *Reader*, §3.1.6 'Vocation of two friends'). The second part of these units will be devoted to a detailed discussion of these problems and the doctrinal solutions to them proposed by the Buddha (§§2.1–2.9.3 below). In this first part we are concerned only with what happened to the Dhamma preached by the Founder in the hands of his disciples: its expression in sacred scriptures and its authority in the eyes of the faithful.

### 1.3.2 The composition of the scriptures

When a Master has taught for forty-five years without ever writing anything down his teaching may be compared to an 'ocean' or a 'forest'. On the death of the Buddha the disciples found themselves confronted with such an ocean or forest. A late text recounts that two of them, who were endowed with exceptional memory, were able to recite the Master's teaching: one concentrating on the disciplinary rules (Vinaya) and the other on his doctrinal preaching (Dhamma). In reality the creation of the Canon of the Buddhist Scriptures was a much more complex event, occurring over a considerable time. It was marked by more than one unexpected turn of events.

1.3.2.1 If a passage in the Canon itself (Vinaya II, 284–308) is to be believed, the first agreed version of the Scriptures was arrived at during the Council called at Rajgir (Rājagaha) shortly after the Founder's death. Kāsyapa, one of the most important monks, seems to have possessed qualities of leadership. Alarmed at certain too-liberal proclamations he wished to prevent indiscipline and error from infiltrating the monastic order. Consequently, he proposed that they should recite together, in order to fix them, once and for all, the Dhamma and the Vinaya. For this purpose a Council of 500 monks met at Rajgir (cf. *Encyclopedia*, p. 264). The two monks endowed with exceptional memory were called upon. One, called Upāli, supplied abundant information about the Vinaya; the other, called Ānanda, about the Dhamma. After discussion the texts were approved. However the Council was later joined by a further group of 500 monks. The leader of the newcomers expressed reservations about the texts already approved. He wished to preserve the Dhamma such as he himself had heard it from the mouth of the Buddha. (The full story is complicated: a great many details and discussions have been omitted here. You may gain further particulars of these and subsequent developments by reading *Ling*, §3.2.)

1.3.2.2 Similar differences of opinion were again apparent in the Council of Vesālī (although we may follow one of the accounts in assuming this Council to have taken place a century after the Buddha's death, little is really known about it—neither the date, the location nor the participants). These divisions became much more marked 116 years after the death of the Buddha, when one of the movements known as the Great Assembly (*Mahāsangha*), which had perhaps from the start represented majority opinion, separated itself from the First Council (of Rajgir) on several points of doctrine. According to the Mahāsangha a man who became enlightened was still exposed to error, ignorance and doubt. From the debates emerged the two great divisions of the faithful: the doctrine of the Ancients (*Theravāda*), scornfully referred to by

*Figure 7   The Golden Buddha (Phra Bang) displayed in the forecourt of the Temple of War Mai Souvannaphoumaram, Laos. For the last 600 years, the Phra Bang has embodied Laotian sovereignty and its possession has always been a test of royal legitimacy. (Camera Press. Photograph by Lynda Scarth.)*

its detractors as the Lesser Vehicle *Hīnayāna*), and the Great Vehicle (*Mahāyāna*), so called by its supporters.

1.3.2.3 E. Lamotte, one of the greatest historians of Indian Buddhism, has summarized in his *Histoire du Bouddhisme Indien* (vol. 1, p. 154)[1] the conclusions to be drawn from the situation we have outlined:

> In the first century after the Buddha's entry into Nirvāna one or more groups of specialists, whether gathered together in Councils or not, tried to codify the words of the Buddha with regard to both doctrine and discipline. They succeeded in formulating a Law and a Rule which were coherent and accepted in their entirety by the primitive community. These constituted the common heritage of the different Buddhist sects which were to develop later.

1.3.2.4 The multiple development of these sects was due to many factors, notably the distance between the great Buddhist centres and the absence of a firmly established hierarchy. The result of this diversity was the development of the original common heritage in a variety of schools and canons employing different languages. These languages were, in particular, Magadhī (the language of the Buddha's own region); Pali (retained today as the canonical language of southern Buddhism); and classical and Buddhist Sanskrit (in northern Buddhism).

[1] Lamotte, E. (1958) *Histoire du Bouddhisme Indien*, Louvain, Bibliothèque du Muséon.

### 1.3.3 The division of the scriptures

As far as what is called 'the Pali Canon' is concerned we find that the Scriptures are distributed in a 'Triple Basket' (*Tripitaka*). The first of the three Baskets comprises the Rules of conduct, the Discipline (*Vinayapitaka*); the second, doctrinal statements (*Suttapitaka*): the third. collections of later elaborations (*Abhidhammapitaka*) (see *Encyclopedia*, p. 264).

1.3.3.1 The first Basket contains an account of the origins of Buddhism, a detailed explanation of various points of the Public Confession (*uposatha*) used in the communities (see below—Sangha) at regular intervals, both for the monks (*bhikkhu*) and for the nuns (*bhikkhunī*), as well as ordinances governing the ceremonies and activities of monastic life.

1.3.3.2 The second Basket contains five collections (*nikāya*) of doctrinal expositions: long expositions (Dīgha-Nikāya), expositions of medium length (Majjhima-Nikāya), expositions which have been 'joined together' (Samyutta-Nikāya), expositions classified according to a numerical system (Anguttara-Nikāya), and minor expositions (Khuddaka-Nikāya). The allocation of texts to the various collections appears, on occasions, to be rather arbitrary. For instance, it is to be noted that it is in the last collection that one finds some of the most celebrated works in verse, works which are very much part of present-day Buddhism: the Dhammapada, and the Suttanipāta (both quoted extensively in the Course Reader).

1.3.3.3 The third Basket gives a detailed systematic account of the teaching of the *Sūtras*. It includes enumerations, summaries, exposition in question and answer form, etc. If the different schools have Suttapitaka which are practically identical and Vinayapitaka which are rather similar, the same cannot be said of the Abhidhammapitaka—the scholarly expression of their different, even opposite, ways of seeing things. Between these there is only a loose relationship. The most important Abhidhamma that we have are those of the two ancient schools: the Theravādin and the Sarvāstivādin.

### 1.3.4 The authority of the scriptures

Nowadays the authority of the Canon is no longer discussed within the groups which have adopted their particular version. However, the *limits* of the Canon of the Scriptures, especially as far as the Abhidhamma are concerned, may differ according to the various schools. Nevertheless, by virtue of having the same Suttapitaka, all Buddhists share a common stock of presuppositions, of problems and answers to problems, all attributed literally to the Buddha himself. Likewise the translators, notably Chinese, Tibetan and Japanese, manifest an extremely literal fidelity to the original texts. This attitude stems from the unconditional respect shown by all for the words of the Buddha. This guarantees the reliability and the permanence of the basic content. It is this common core of material which will be dealt with in the second section of these units. It is also out of this common core that the movements and schools, to be examined in the third section, developed.

## 1.4  The Community: the Sangha

The Buddha's preaching had quite quickly led to the formation around him of a gathering of followers or a community (*Sangha*). This had certain characteristic attributes, which I shall now describe.

### 1.4.1 Following the Master

1.4.1.1 A band of more or less regular followers gathered around the Buddha during his itinerant preaching. As in the case of all the spiritual leaders in India at this time these followers were of various kinds. There were the seekers after novelty, with plenty of leisure to indulge their curiosity; there were hostile listeners, eager for conflict, at least in words; there were people who had been hurt or disappointed by life; but there were also many sincere and genuine seekers after truth who were satisfied neither by the ritualistic cults of the brāhmaṇs nor by the extreme practices of the ascetics.

1.4.1.2 The latter group became more or less committed to following the Buddha's teaching. Some of them, in a spirit of syncretistic tolerance typical of India, combined their sympathy for Buddhism with continuing attachment to their previous religious allegiances, or with a broad moral perspective of honesty, fraternity and peace. Those who asked to be accepted as disciples had their request granted. As the classical formula puts it, they took refuge in the Buddha, the Dhamma and the Sangha. They were received either by the Master himself who, without formality, told them simply '*ehi*', ('come'), or by one of the great preachers, or by one of the communities. The latter always deliberated before admitting new members.

1.4.1.3 Discipleship could take several forms. Some disciples did not wish or were unable to abandon the life of the world completely, as the Buddha had done. They remained disciples in the world whether they were men (*upāsaka*) or women (*upāsikā*). Their affiliation consisted essentially of observing the five basic prohibitions (of violence, theft, lying, sexual activity contrary to their status, alcohol) and of making offerings of food, clothes and other essentials to the monks to enable them to survive without worries or desires and to concentrate on their sole purpose of working towards spiritual liberation. The lay disciples, it seems, also undertook certain 'devotional' activities: veneration of the Master's relics, visits to temples for meditation, listening to the words of the Buddha read to them by the monks. Some of the lay disciples, out of devotion, adopted practices which were strictly speaking those of the monks. This will be discussed below (see *Ling*, §2.34).

### 1.4.1.4 Exercise

Now for an exercise to reflect upon Buddhist morality. For this read the passage 'Good conduct', *Reader*, §3.2.7 and also *Reader*, §3.4.7, which gives the text of Aśoka's Thirteenth Rock Edict. What do these passages show us about Buddhist morality?

PLEASE PAUSE HERE

DO NOT READ ON UNTIL YOU HAVE COMPLETED THE EXERCISE

### 1.4.1.5 Specimen answer and discussion

Morality is one of the three parts of the spiritual training of a Buddhist (the other two being meditation and wisdom). A virtuous life is the basis of all other achievements. For layfolk, men and women, obedience to the Five Precepts, which are common to many Indian ascetical groups, will ensure a good or better karma and hence progress in the long journey, extending over many lives, to *Nirvāna*. Numbers 9 and 10 of the precepts of good conduct are clearly for monks only. Numbers 6 and 7 are intended to secure a peaceful and harmonious social life. Buddhism lays great stress on non-violence. Aśoka's Rock Edict shows the impact of such teachings upon a king, and suggests what a powerful effect such an ethic could have upon political behaviour. (Perhaps, however, it should be added, in this context, that Buddhist ideas of non-violence did not prevent many Buddhist kings of India and Ceylon from becoming great conquerors and pursuing their political aims with much the same ruthlessness as their Hindu neighbours.) Note, however, that it is not easy to identify in this edict of Aśoka what are specifically Buddhist precepts, as distinct from general broadly-based ethical principles, already traditional in Indian religious culture. The word 'Law' (Dharma), for instance, may be taken in a general sense or in peculiarly Buddhist sense (see §1.3.1 above). Regret for past violent acts comes into the same category. The desire for peace and happiness for all beings, the preoccupation with assuring happiness in a future life or lives by doing good in this world—these are general human aspirations as well as being Buddhist principles.

### 1.4.2  Becoming a monk

1.4.2.1  Nevertheless the only complete and logical Buddhist is the monk, for he renounces his worldly goods, even his own individuality, leading a celibate and continent life, stripped of all property, in order to destroy within himself all desire. He aims at an ever stricter discipline, a more and more enlightened meditation in order, in this way, to attain liberation from suffering.

The renunciation of the world for spiritual purposes was very much part of the Indian tradition. The classical pattern was for a man, after going through the stages of upbringing in youth, and then of fatherhood of a family in order to ensure the continuation of his line, eventually to become a hermit in the forest and then a wandering ascetic. Buddhism was only following this tradition when it called for renunciation. This abandonment of the world could occur as early as at the age of eight but the candidate could only be fully received into the monastic community at the age of twenty, after a demanding period of apprenticeship and scrutiny. Now read the passages 'Two kinds of quest' (*Reader*, §3.2.6) and 'Show me an island' (*Reader*, §3.2.8).

1.4.2.2  Entry into a monastery, after the abandonment of the world, was not necessarily understood as being binding for life. It might only be a question of a kind of 'spiritual period' intended to lead to the attainment of enlightenment or, at least, to various forms of spiritual progress. In practice, as Buddhism developed and established itself, often under the protection of the ruling powers, the monasteries became not only centres of spiritual activity but of organized study of all kinds, including literature and art and the general education of the laity, both adults and children. Thus it became normal practice in certain periods and certain countries for someone seeking education and other refinements (and, moreover, seeking to acquire merit for himself and his family) to spend weeks, months or years in a monastery. It was quite regular, therefore, for the monastic profession to be temporary.

1.4.2.3  However, the most earnest monks made, and still make today, a long-term and even permanent commitment. The quest for liberation is an onerous task; it represents a long and difficult path taking up an entire life, or sometimes several lives if one is not enough. In such a case it is only in another existence, either on earth or in some paradise, that present efforts will be rewarded and that full liberation will be achieved—if the one who seeks it has merited it by his faithfulness.

Figure 8   Tonsure, Taiwan. (Photography by Prof. H. Welch. Reproduced from H. Welch (1967) The Practise of Chinese Buddhism 1900–1950, Harvard University Press. Copyright © by the President and Fellows of Harvard College.)

(a)  The disciple, wearing a business suit, enters behind his master.

(b)  He offers incense at the main·altar.

(c)  He kneels at a side altar.

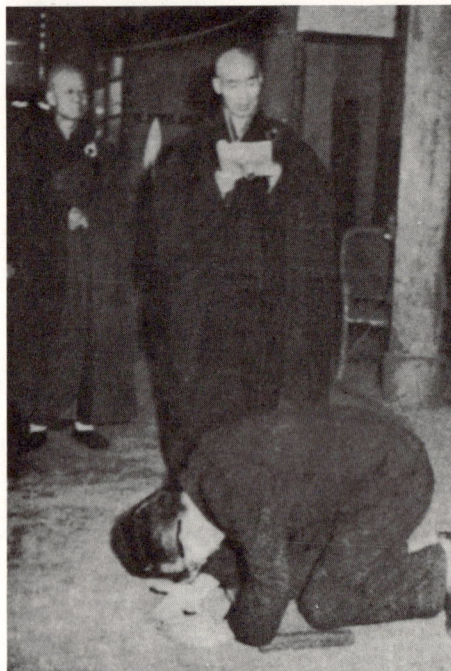

(d)  He makes a last kowtow to his parents.

(e)  His master sprinkles him with holy water.

(f)  He offers his master a razor.

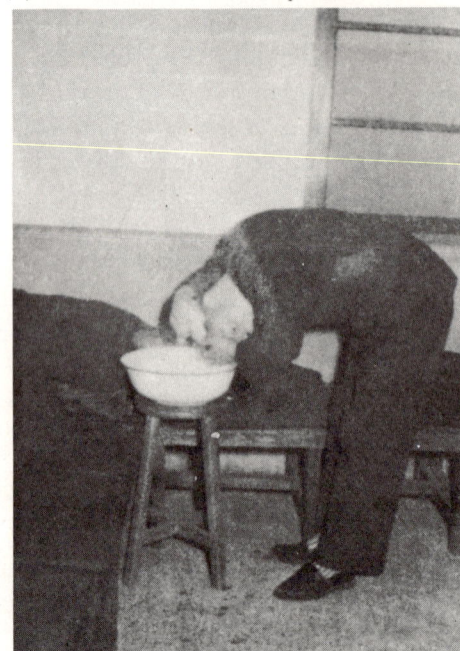

(g)  He shampoos his own head.

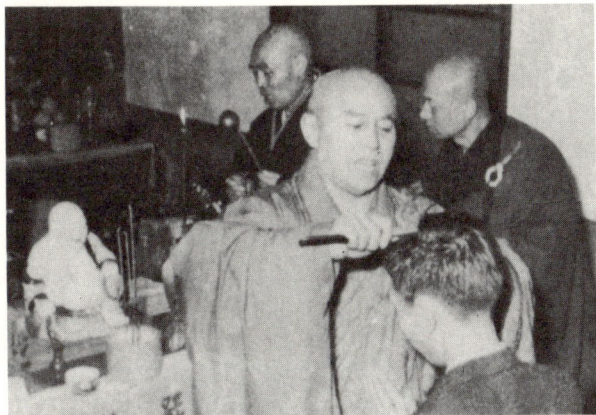

(h) His master shaves off the hair on the sides of his head.

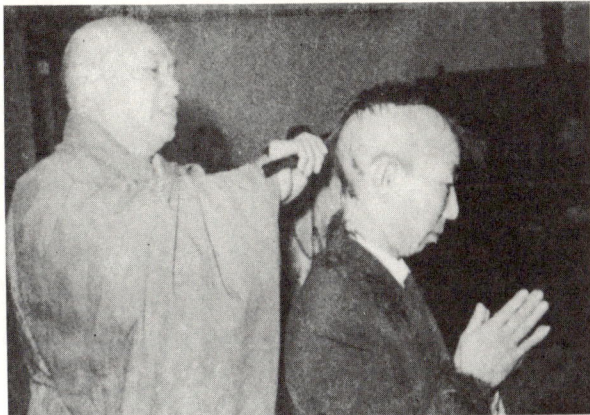

(i) His master shaves off the last tuft.

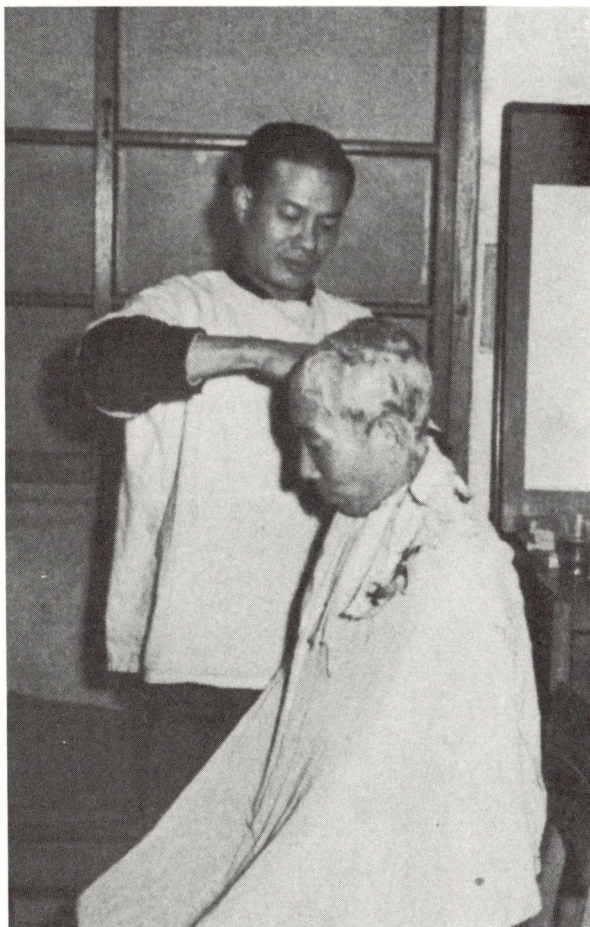

(j) The barber finishes the shaving.

(k) The disciple stands before the altar.

(l) He offers incense.

(m) With family and friends.

### 1.4.3  Living in the community

Originally Buddhist monastic life seems to have been developed by, and for, men only. It was only after a certain time, on the insistence of devout women in his family, and with considerable reluctance, that the Buddha allowed the creation of female communities. He gave them (or they were given later) about twice as many rules as the monks and they were subject to male authority. The oldest and most advanced nun had to recognize the authority of the youngest monk or even an inexperienced novice.

It is customary for Buddhists to be classified in four categories (*parisad*) given in descending order of dignity: monks, nuns, laymen, laywomen. To become a monk is the supreme undertaking.

1.4.3.1  As soon as a monk has taken on the outward attributes of shaven head, shaven beard and yellow robe he is also subject to the ten prohibitions (or precepts). Besides the five he observes in common with the laity (see §1.4.1 above) he abstains from eating outside prescribed times; from taking part in or being present at dancing, musical activities or entertainments generally; he must not use garlands, perfumes or unguents; he must not have an over-comfortable bed; finally, he must not possess nor handle gold or silver (see *Reader*, §3.3.2 'The Ten Precepts').

1.4.3.2  As soon as his renunciation of the world (*pravrajyā*) has been formalized, the candidate commences a period of training under the direction of a tutor, whose accommodation he shares, and a spiritual master (*ācārya*) whose pupil he becomes. Throughout this period he remains a novice (*shrāmanera*). His time is spent in the service of his tutor, in religious studies, the acquisition of some areas of secular knowledge and in training for the various aspects of life in the community.

1.4.3.3  When he is ready, his ordination ceremony requires an assembly of monks (at least five, or ten), who conduct an examination of the candidate (see *Reader*, §3.3.1 'The scrutiny of admission to the order'). Then the master of ceremonies asks the members of the assembly three times if they think the postulant should be accepted; their silence is the indication of an affirmative response. Once the candidate has been accepted, he puts on the monastic robes again and a note is made of the day and the time of the ceremony which will determine his place in the order of precedence within the community.

### 1.4.4  Life as a monk

1.4.4.1  As his name indicates the *bhikku* is a mendicant monk whose possessions are limited and whose subsistence is provided, in theory, only by the generosity of lay persons. He has three garments: the inner, the outer and his cloak. His other 'possessions' are a bowl for collecting gifts of food, a filter for water, a toothpick, a razor, a needle, a stick and a fan. All these objects are returned to the community if he should leave the monastery or upon his death.

1.4.4.2  The monk lives on food (usually balls of rice) which he has to seek in the form of alms each morning. This must be consumed by midday. Butter, ghee (melted butter), oil, honey and sugar are considered as medicaments only to be given to the sick. Meat and fish are eaten very exceptionally and then only when it is clear that the animal has not been killed specially in order to provide food for the monk. (This would be regarded as an infringement of the first precept.)

*Figure 9  Meditation Hall in a Buddhist monastery, Japan. (Japanese Information Service.)*

*Figure 10  Prayer before a meal in a Buddhist monastery, Japan. (Japanese Information Service.)*

(a)

(b)

(c)

*Figure 11 Kenheri caves near Bombay (a) hillside entrance; (b)carved figures near entrance; (c) another view of carved figures; (d) entrance to one of the cave temples; (e) figure of Buddha. The photographs show three of the one hundred and nine Buddhist carves carved in a hillside set in jungle. Some caves are solitary cells (a), others are grand affairs with magnificent carvings (d, e). Photographs (b) (note the jungle outside the cave entrance) and (c) show a pleasant compromise. The caves were used by both Therevāda and Mahāyāna Buddhists, and were occupied from the second century BC to the ninth century CE. They are fine examples of one of the most striking features of Indian art, the rock-cut temple. For the precise location of these caves see Unit 28, Figure 6(a). (John R. Hinnells.)*

23

1.4.4.3 At first the dwelling-places of the monks were temporary and improvised. They lived beneath trees, in caves, in huts made of leaves. Later, monasteries of wood, brick and stone were built which became, with the passage of time, vast complexes, often of architectural merit. Originally, the choice between a fixed abode and the itinerant life was decided partly according to individual preference and partly according to the cycle of the seasons. Whereas one could travel freely in the dry months, movement was impossible during the monsoon rains.

1.4.4.4 As the great monasteries become numerous and the communal life of large numbers of monks clearly necessitated a fixed routine, a set order was given to the day. The monks rise very early and wash before meditation. Then they get dressed for going outside to seek gift-offerings of food each morning from the lay believers. They return to the monastery to wash off the dust accumulated during this exercise and to eat. The masters then give spiritual instruction to the disciples before the period of spiritual and physical rest during the hot part of the day which lasts until about 4 pm. After this rest those monks who are qualified for the task make themselves available to the public and participate in consultations and discussions. When nightfall comes the monks return to the monastery. The evening bath is followed by the final discussion of the day as the disciples gather around the masters.

1.4.4.5 The year is punctuated by a variety of ceremonies. Twice a month, the monks gather for a day of confession and expiation of faults (*uposatha*). The most notable celebration, ever since ancient times, has been the 'going out from the retreat' at the end of the rainy season; it marks the recommencement of travel and preaching.

1.4.4.6 The community is a brotherhood of 'solitary monks who live together'. Discipline is the result of voluntary consent and is derived partly from tradition and from the occasional decisions of authority. This authority is recognized by all as necessary within reasonable limits and is exercized by a Superior assisted by a Council and, to some extent, by consultations with the entire community. Harmonious co-existence is the greatest boon of the community but is also sometimes one of the most easily upset. (Read here 'The welfare of a community' *Reader*, §3.3.5).

1.4.4.7 Before he died the Buddha had said: 'After me your Master will be the Doctrine itself'. But as soon as groups became established, there was a call for this fundamental authority to be interpreted by others—at least on a local level. On a wider scale, beyond the groups and local federations of monasteries (*nikāya*), which might appoint leaders (*nayaka*), as in Ceylon, no one has ever, in the history of Buddhism, thought of proclaiming himself as a universal spiritual leader. Nor has it even been thought that such a leader could be necessary. This fact explains in part the diversity, even the opposition, between certain doctrinal currents and practical devotions within Buddhism, and the multiplicity of schools and observances.

Nevertheless it is undeniable that beneath this diversity there subsists a common and universal desire to be faithful to the basic Doctrine (which will be discussed in §2) regarded as occupying the place of the Master. This common desire has, however, led historically to quite different conclusions, as will be seen in §3.

1.4.4.8 Such then, is the Assembly, the Community, the Sangha. It has survived for 2,500 years. Like any human group it has its heroes as well as many decent, honourable people; it has also its dullards, its slackers, even its profiteers. But it remains an impressive testimony to the unrelenting spiritual search of millions of men scandalized by the existence of suffering. They have sought to understand its workings, to circumvent its effects and to attain the light of spiritual wisdom, the peace of liberation. Their guiding light remains the one who was first Enlightened beneath the fig tree. (Now read 'The wise and thoughtful Bhikkhu', *Reader*, §3.3.4.)

## 1.5 The Buddhist and the Three Jewels

### 1.5.1 Authority

Buddhism was born out of the experience of the Buddha, demonstrated subsequently in his teaching. This teaching has been preserved in texts which are believed to be authentic and the substance and expression of which have been fixed in various canonical scriptures, translated into several languages—in particular, in the Pali Canon, safeguarded by the monks of Sri Lanka and southern Buddhism generally. In his lifetime the Buddha sought and obtained, through the confidence his disciples had in him, the status of a definitive and infallible Master. The literal interpretation of the Canon, which is his teaching, rests on these same two qualities.

### 1.5.2 Experience

Yet it would be wrong to think that the Buddha and the Scriptures are to be accepted by the believer with an immediate, permanent and unquestioning faith. In reality, the Buddha himself indicated several times how his message was to be accepted and treated. Certainly, from the very start it should be approached with the immense respect accorded to a discovery of capital importance; with a great trust in one who, 'having succeeded thus' (*Tathāgata*), speaks of what he has himself experienced in a decisive fashion. It should be approached with willingness to accept the basic axioms which he proclaims (*Reader*, §3.1.4 and the first three Noble Truths); with willingness to accept the practical Path of which he indicates the eight parts (fourth Noble Truth); and with willingness to accept the practical precepts proposed by him (and subsequently by the community), and which are obligatory for monks.

Nevertheless, the Buddha repeated several times that the seeker after truth, the man engaged in a spiritual quest, must only accept these things provisionally, on condition that they are verified for each individual through his own experience. No message expressed in words can be its own justification—it can be 'proved' only when the person who has heard it and applied it finds that he is indeed led by it to what was promised: the extinction of desire in the midst of the true light which produces (or is) *Nirvāna*.

### 1.5.3 The need for personal discovery

The Buddha always refused to give his disciples any dispensation from the personal effort, reflection and discovery which no one else could undertake on their behalf. He never sought to submit other spiritual seekers unconditionally to his own teaching. He has left to his followers this last demand for freedom: 'Be, each one of you, your own island, your own refuge; do not seek another refuge. It is in this way that you will reach the high place of the Immortal.' (Dīgha-Nikāya, II, p. 100).

### 1.5.4 The need for discipleship

And yet, as we have seen, discipleship remains central. When a man wants to become a Buddhist the formula which he pronounces (either using the actual words or an equivalent) affirms that he is taking refuge not only in the Doctrine (dhamma) verified by his own experience, but also in the Buddha and in the Community (see *Reader*, §3.3.3 'Four fundamental attitudes of a noble disciple'). He must take refuge in the Community, inasmuch as it intends to remain faithful to the spirit and to the words of the Founder, entrusted to the Community. We shall return later to consideration of the role which the Founder has played in the life of practising Buddhists over the centuries. For the moment one must at least indicate here the fundamental place which he occupies permanently in the lives of the faithful in general. He is the *First* who exploited and opened up, by his own efforts, a new way. On this account he remains for all those who have come after him, the *Model*, which one must always seek to emulate. Through his message he is the *Master* whose teachings have shown and prepared the path to be taken. He is *Infallible* and may be followed in hope and without fear (see *Reader*, §3.6.2 'Infallibility of the Buddha').

# 2 HUMAN DESTINY ACCORDING TO CLASSICAL BUDDHISM

## 2.1 The theatre of the world

According to the ancient religious traditions of India (taken over in this respect by Buddhism) the number of universes is infinite, whether existing simultaneously or in succession. In these pages, where we are looking at the cosmos strictly from the Buddhist point of view, it will be enough to consider this universe, *here and now*—the one in which the Buddha lived, in which Buddhism as a movement finds itself, the one in which we ourselves live.

### 2.1.1 The three 'storeys' of the Buddhist universe

The most concrete description of this universe, (again adopted from previous tradition) distinguishes three 'storeys'.

2.1.1.1 The *first* of these worlds is *above the surface of the earth*. This itself consists of several levels, according to the differing degree of sublimity of the 'radiant beings' (that is the meaning of the word *deva*, often translated as 'gods') which are to be found there. (See the explanation in Horner's article, *Encyclopedia*, p. 292, second note.) Thus one can enumerate the following hierarchy, proceeding from the lower to the higher:

(i)   seven minor groups, of which the highest is the class of Brahmā *deva*;

(ii)  four higher groups of 'gods of light' (abhā);

(iii) four groups at a yet higher level, of 'gods of bliss' (subhā);

(iv)  at the summit there are some dozen groups of *deva* at a higher level still. (Majjhima-Nikāya, II, p. 100f)[1]

2.1.1.2 *Secondly* there is the *earth* which is in the form of a disc. In its centre it is dominated by a mythical mountain, higher than all others, called Meru or Sumeru. No doubt the idea was suggested to the Indians by the sight of the Himalayan range. This mountain is surrounded by water on all sides. The earth is divided into four continents, of which one, Janbudvipa, includes India. The ocean which surrounds the earth is also divided into four seas. (*Anguttara-Nikāya*, I, p. 227f, and III, p. 240)

2.1.1.3 At a *third* and lower stage are the *worlds beneath the earth*. There dwell the *Asuras*, who are a kind of Titans, formerly rivals of the gods for dominion over the universe but conquered by them and thrust down into the ocean or into abysses. More important, there is a series of *hells*. There are seven of these, becoming more and more terrible as they go down in descending order. There demons torment those humans who have fallen into perdition. These wretched men are pierced with red-hot swords, hacked to pieces, boiled, roasted, and subjected to other forms of torment. Buddhist imagination has given itself free rein in this sphere, while hastening to add

---

[1] Where, as here, I give supporting references to texts in the Buddhist scriptures which are not included in the *Reader*, it does not mean that you are expected to seek out these texts now. Some students may wish to have such further references for later study. For these passages I usually give the name of the scriptural text, and the page number in the relevant volume of the editions of the Pali Text Society; in a few cases I refer to other editions of texts. Where a text is included in the course *Reader*, I will, as in the first part, continue to give the relevant section reference.

*Figure 12 Mandala of Amitayus. (Courtesy of the Newark Museum (Holton Collection), Newark, New Jersey.)*

that in spite of all these torments the victims are not destroyed: they remain in existence and continue to endure until they have completely expiated their evil past. You will find a vivid description of the infernal torments in *Reader* §3.2.2 'Duration and pains of Hell'. (Other relevant scriptural texts are the Kokaliya Sutta of Suttanipāta; Dhammapada, verse 126; Milindaphañha, III, 4, quoted in *Buddhism in Translations*,[1] pp. 253 ff.)

### 2.1.2 The three spiritual states

Another division of the universe refers to the same constitutive elements as those we have just described, but looks rather to the '*spiritual state*' corresponding to each level of existence. From this point of view, we must distinguish between three planes (*dhātu*) or domains (*avacāra*). In ascending order, they are as follows:

2.1.2.1 The *lowest plane* is that of *concupiscence* (*kāma*) and it includes all who are subject to the law of sexual desire. Beginning from the deepest hell, this

[1] Warren, H. C. (1909) *Buddhism in Translations*, Harvard University Press.

28

plane includes the demons, the inhabitants of hell, the shades (see §2.2.1 below), then animals and men, and extends upwards as far as the sixth of the seven groups of minor gods mentioned above §2.1.1.1. All beings in this plane have a nature composed of five elements *(khandha)*: *vedāna* (feelings), *saññā* (perceptions), *sankārā* (volitional or habitual mental tendencies), *viññāna* (consciousness), *rūpa* (bodily form).

2.1.2.2 Next there is the *plane of forms (rūpa-dhātu)*, inhabited by a certain number of higher gods proceeding upwards from the seventh group of minor gods. Like those in the previous category, they too are made up of the same five elements; but they are freed from concupiscence, although they retain a perceptible form.

2.1.2.3 The highest gods of all have neither concupiscence nor even a form *(rūpa)* which is perceptible by the senses. They are in the *plane of formlessness (arūpa-dhātu)*. (Traditional Buddhist wisdom is more or less agreed on the constitution of the three planes I have just described.) In the *Reader* §3.2.1, you will find a late text, there entitled 'The thirty-one grades of beings in the universe'. It gives a more complicated description, and you will see that it does not correspond neatly with the structure of the universe that I have summarized above, from the canonical texts. But it is worth reading this picturesque account, and comparing it with the elements in my summary.

2.1.2.4 Still higher than these planes, or rather in a different order of reality, Buddhists speak of the *plane of Nirvāna*. It is to this that the Buddhas have arrived, so escaping from all the preceding categories.

### 2.1.3 Buddhist art and the theatre of the world

Buddhist art represents this 'theatre of the world' through various art forms.

2.1.3.1 In Tibet there are symbolic representations called *mandala*. These provide a kind of 'geographical map' of the universe with all the beings in it. These figures have a circular pattern, divided into six segments, according to the six categories of beings who are involved in the universal drama.

2.1.3.2 In the countries of South-East Asia, the structure of the universe is symbolically represented in the very design to which certain great temples have been built. Their ascending terraces, piled one above the other, becoming narrower as they go higher and higher, represent the different levels of the universe from the lowest to the highest. We find huge edifices expressing this kind of concept at Borobudur in Java and Angkor-Wat in Cambodia. The faithful pilgrim, mounting the succession of staircases, making his way along the terraces and gazing on the host of statues, acquires a conception of the vast world swarming with living beings.

## 2.2 The actors on the stage

We have already said something about the actors on this universal stage. The living beings *(sattva)* are found to be divided into the following categories, according to their respective destinies.

### 2.2.1 Demons, the doomed and the shades

Lowest of all are *the demons*, who seem to be fixed for ever in their role of

*Figure 13  Aerial view of Angkor Wat. (Mansell Collection.)*

*Figure 14  South West view of Angkor Wat. (École Française d'Extrème Orient, Paris.)*

torturers. Their victims, *the doomed*, inhabit the same infernal regions. They have been brought to their wretched estate by their evil actions previously committed. 'Neither in the air above, nor in the depths of the sea, nor by hiding yourself in the deepest cleft of the mountains, nor in any other part of the world, will you ever find a place where you can escape from the consequences of your evil actions' (Dhammapada, 127). 'The fool (i.e. he who has not listened to and accepted the message of the Buddha and acted accordingly), after the disintegration of the elements which make up his being, falls into hell' (*ibid.*, 140).

Also in the sub-terrestrial world, there is the ill-defined abode of *the shades of the dead (preta)*. These wandering, famished wraiths are seeking new forms which will make it possible for them to become reborn.

### 2.2.2 Nāgas, animals and human beings

We come now to the terrestrial regions. We need not discuss here the world of plants, since Buddhism does not include the latter among living beings. First there are *the animals*, from the smallest to the greatest, from the most harmless to the most malign. Among these are included various more-or-less 'deified animals', such as the nāgas, mythical serpents which can change themselves into men, and which protect Buddhas and Buddhists generally.

Also on this earth are *human beings* in all their diversity. (Buddhism is aware of the problem of human inequality, and we find the classical texts asking the reason for it (see below, §§2.3.2.4–2.3.2.5). Buddhism views mankind from a viewpoint of sombre realism. It sees men as beings marked out for death. It takes pains to describe their growing old, their illnesses, their death throes, and their subsequent corruption.

### 2.2.3 The Asura

Situated at different levels (about which it is hard to be precise) are the *Asura* (see §2.1.1.3 above). In the Buddhist universe they play an ambiguous role, which is sometimes positive and sometimes negative. In any case, it is a relatively minor role.

### 2.2.4 The deva

2.2.4.1 At the summit of all are the *deva*, the 'radiant beings', gods or godlings. They are assured of a longer life, and of a happier destiny than the common run of mortals. However, for them too there is an eventual decease, and they too must be reborn. 'The thirty three gods and the gods of Yama, the gods who enjoy their own transformations and the sovereign gods, linked by the chain of desire (a desire which is not fleshly but real all the same) fall back into the power of Evil' (Samyutta-Nikāya, I, p. 133). In the sacred Scriptures of Buddhism there are many accounts of intervention by the deva in the world. However, these deva are evidently inferior to the Buddhas, and like all other living beings, they must learn from the Buddha the secret of salvation.

### 2.2.4.2 Question

It is sometimes said that Buddhism is 'atheist'. Since we are here discussing the destiny of man, according to Buddhist belief, this a suitable place, after the discussion in the preceding paragraphs, to ask whether you think that the term 'atheist' is rightly applied to the Buddha and to the religious movement which he founded.

PLEASE PAUSE HERE

DO NOT READ ON UNTIL YOU HAVE COMPLETED THE EXERCISE

### 2.2.4.3 Specimen answer and discussion

More usually, the term 'atheist' means that one definitely denies the existence of a god. It can also refer to the view of one who feels no interest in or need for a god. From his whole doctrine, and from certain explicit texts, it seems that the Buddha always refused to answer Yes or No when he was asked 'questions which do not help spiritual progress'. For him, it was a useless question to deliberate about the existence of the gods. Such a question is irrelevant to the sole concern of man, as the Buddha explained it. No one can save a man, except the man himself. If there are gods, they themselves are in need of working out their own liberation, by hearing and accepting the Noble Truths of Buddhism. However, as we shall see below, in later Buddhism a certain transcendence, and a certain abiding power and influence for men's liberation, came to be attributed to the Founder himself.

You may think, from the frequent mention of the deva, a word which is often translated as 'gods', that it is evident that Buddhism is not 'atheist' in the sense of denying the existence of gods. However, as Horner notes (in *Encyclopedia*, p. 292) it is misleading to translate the word deva as 'god, angel, divine or celestial being'. And 'in no sense is a deva a creator, omnipotent or omniscient, but simply a denizen of a deva-world'.

## 2.3 The forces involved in the drama

### 2.3.1 The Indian attitude to salvation

There are three points we should note in particular if we wish to distinguish the Indian attitude (whether Hindu or Buddhist) to the problem of salvation, from other religious perspectives—for example, from those of Christianity or of Islam.

2.3.1.1 *First:* None of the states of being described above in §2.2 is absolutely final. All beings, not excepting the deva, are subject to a progressive 'wearing out'—to old age, to death, and to return in a new state. In principle, this process continues without end, since all existence, according to the law of karma (see §2.3.2 below), produces fruits which must have their due consequences in a following existence. The 'wheel' of rebirths is set to turn endlessly. The Buddha's claim was precisely to give a method to enable one to break out of this closed circle and to halt the process for oneself.

2.3.1.2 *Secondly:* Likewise, no death is final. After a longer or shorter interval, everyone is *born again* in a new existence. Moreover, this new existence is also provisional, leading on to death.

2.3.1.3 *Thirdly,* and above all: In this process, the beings who are reborn are *not necessarily in the same kind of existence* in which they were situated previously. On the contrary, they would be more often than not at a different level of existence. So it happens that men become animals, or deva, or demons; demons pass to the state of human life: and deva fall to our level, or even lower.[1]

### 2.3.2 Karma and the destiny of man

2.3.2.1 Limiting ourselves for a moment to man's standpoint, let us ask *why* a man ascends to heaven, or goes down to hell, why is he reborn in a higher or lower form of existence than before. In general, the reply is: he ascends or goes down according to the merits or demerits acquired during the previous period of existence. Here read the fourth passage in *Reader* §3.2.3 'Rebirth–Samsara: What follows after him?'.

2.3.2.2 To illustrate this law, Buddhism has recourse to an analogy with the

---

[1] One text (admittedly a rare example), tells of a frog which, because it heard the Buddha preaching just before a cowherd crushed it with his stick, was reborn immediately in heaven among the gods! (Visuddhi-Magga, VII; see Warren, H. C. (1909) *op. cit.*

productive life of plants. The Buddha made use of it in speaking to his monks:

> Consider a healthy seed, which has been suitably sown in well-prepared soil in a fertile field; if the rain falls at the right time, the seed will germinate, spring up and develop. Exactly in the same way, whatever may be the present standing of a man, his actions will ripen and he will have to experience their fruit, whether in this life or in another.

> (Anguttara-Nikāya, III p. 33; see Warren, *ibid.* p. 216).

Thus each action, according to its good or evil quality, produces *seeds*, whether useful or poisonous, which bear within themselves a future either of happiness or of misery. They come to germinate and to ripen, and to bring forth corresponding fruits. The man who was the author of these actions must then experience the consequences, either of happiness or of misery. He may do so in this present life, or if he does not 'eat the fruit' now, he must do so in a further existence. This law was already accepted in pre-Buddhist religious culture (see *Ling*, §1.32). Buddhism has always believed and affirmed the same law. (Here read the first passage in *Reader*, §3.2.3 'Rebirth–Samsara: The round of existence.')

2.3.2.3 As you have seen in the preceeding units on Hinduism, the technical term corresponding to this analogy is *karma*. This word, which comes from the root *kri* in the Sanskrit language (which is related to our word *create*), means to act, to produce a result in a certain field of activity. Here it means to prepare future retribution by means of one's present actions. Thus in the last resort karma is the force which may determine the whole destiny of man. Buddhism seems to have understood this law in a universal sense.

2.3.2.4 As far as material consequences are concerned its application is obvious. When the king Milinda asked the reason for human inequalities, the sage Nagasena replied by using the analogy of different forms of plant life, which from different seeds produce different fruits. You will find this dialogue between the two in the *Reader*, in the last passage in §3.2.3 'Rebirth–Samsara: The cause of inequality among living men'. See also *Reader*, §3.2.4 'Fruitful and barren karma'.

2.3.2.5 In the text referred to, giving Nagasena's reply to the king, the writer goes on to add another difference, attributing to karma the reason why some men are wise and others are foolish. This of course, raises a problem. If even one's *moral attitude* itself, which is going to determine the quality of one's future acts, is purely the automatic result of past acts, what room is there for human freedom and the possibility of 'changing' one's life?

The texts do not all give the same answer to this question. Sometimes they explain the present wickedness of a man by a preceding karma which he cannot resist. Sometimes, on the other hand, it seems that the Buddha regards man as free, truly holding his destiny in his own hands, capable of directing this destiny. In particular, man is considered capable of choosing conversion to Buddhism, or of persevering in faithfulness to it in spite of temptation. More than once, the Master appeals to the free choice of his hearers. He challenges them with the classical and very simple formula of the ancient texts: *ehi*—'come'.

### 2.3.2.6 Exercise
As an exercise to revise the matter dealt with in §2.2 and §2.3, write your own explanation of this passage from the Dhammapada:

All that we are is the result of what we have thought: it is founded on our thoughts and made up of our thoughts. If a man speaks or acts with an evil thought, suffering follows him, as the wheel follows the hoof of the bullock that draws the cart.

Before you write your comments, it will help you to read reflectively through Horner's treatment of karma and its consequences in the *Encyclopedia*, pp. 274–9.

PLEASE PAUSE HERE

DO NOT READ ON UNTIL YOU HAVE COMPLETED THE EXERCISE

### 2.3.2.7 Specimen answer

When the Dhammapada speaks of 'thoughts', it does not mean intellectual considerations, but a general attitude of 'desire' or of 'no-desire' towards existing realities. 'Thoughts' are evil when they create or increase in men the desires which cause sorrow, and lead to further rebirths. One sees here an expression of the universality of the law of karma. According to this law, retribution can take place in this life, or in another life, when rebirth may occur either in the form of an animal, or in hell, or as a deva (see above §§2.2.1–2.2.4).

## 2.4   Man in himself and under karma

### 2.4.1   The conditions of the nature of Man

Man is subject to karma, like all other beings according to the conditions of his nature. Now we must say a little more precisely what those conditions are.

Buddhists hold that man is the compound result of a material component and a mental component.

### 2.4.2   The material component

The material component is the body (*kāya*); obviously, it is materially extended in three dimensions, and it is endowed with *six* senses. There are the five senses which Western tradition acknowledges, and a sixth sense called *Manas*, which groups the perceptions of the five other senses to give a complete representation of the object perceived. The body, with its inclinations and its activities, is not regarded in Buddhism. The body is accused of dragging man downwards towards the material sphere—especially towards sexual temptations. Moreover, it is considered to have no substantial solidity, as witness its decomposition after death. Now look at *Reader*, §3.4.2 'Reflections on the worthlessness of the body'.

### 2.4.3   The mental component

The mental component in man is manifested in all the activities which are not limited to the senses: those activities which we call intellectual, and which Buddhism groups in categories of five principal activities, which we need not discuss in detail here. We may think it natural to conclude that, since there are mental activities, there is also a mind, an 'I', as a permanent reality. We shall see that Buddhists hold exactly the contrary: what you may call mind and what you may believe to be a lasting 'I' is only a collection of fortuitous and disconnected acts. It is pointless to say, 'It's mine'; pointless to say, 'It's I'; pointless to say 'It's myself'. The sage Nagasena gave an arresting analogy to illustrate this fundamental conviction, in a passage reproduced in the *Reader*, §3.2.5 'There is no ego'.

### 2.4.3.1 Exercise

In the light of these texts and of the passages in Horner's sections on 'The five khandhā' and 'The not-self' (*Encyclopedia*, pp. 279–82), write a comment on this other text of the Dhammapada: 'The fool thinks anxiously: "These sons and this wealth are mine". But he is not even master of himself, much less of sons and goods'.

PLEASE PAUSE HERE<br>
DO NOT READ ON UNTIL YOU HAVE COMPLETED THE EXERCISE

### 2.4.3.2 Specimen answer

The text speaks of a 'fool', a man subject to infatuation, illusion, stupidity (*moha*). Such a man thinks things are real and belong to him. More in depth: he thinks that he himself is a permanent and substantial reality, when, in fact, he is only an accidental aggregate of elements. There is no 'ego'; therefore nothing can 'belong' to it. When a man has discovered that, he will not be attached to or have a desire for any object, not even for his own experience—whether for his body or for his spiritual elements.

## 2.5  The realm of suffering

### 2.5.1  Life as an illusion

Thus, when we affirm the existence of our own personality, we are living in an illusion. Buddhism makes its position here precise by saying: Everything that we believe makes up solid realities is only impermanent, only insubstantial, only a source of sorrow and pain. These three qualities—impermanence, insubstantiality, and sorrow are the three characteristics of human life and of the drama in which it is lived. Let us consider them in turn.

### 2.5.2  Impermanence, insubstantiality and sorrow

2.5.2.1 One of the most famous Buddhist axioms is stated in three words: *Sabbe saṅkharā aniccā*—all that is composite is *impermanent*. In everyday language, nothing that is 'put together' can last. An early text, attributed to the Founder, predicts the progressive dissolution of the world in which we live, using as an illustration the terrible droughts of India:[1]

---

[1] The description of the destruction of the world appears in many texts, for instance: Dīrgha-āgama, Lokaprajñapatisūtra; also in Visuddhi-Magga, chapter XIII, translated in *The Path of Purity*, London, Pali Text Society, vol. II pp. 48f., and in Warren, H. C. (1909) *ibid.*, pp. 321f.

There will come a time when the rains will fall no longer and when all the plants, the trees and the other vegetation will be dried up and destroyed. A second sun will appear, and then the streams and the brooks will run dry. When a third sun appears, the great rivers, even the most important of all—even Ganges and Yamunā—they too will run dry. The mountains, even the highest, and the whole of this earth itself, will begin to smoke and will be consumed in a great and universal holocaust ... So impermanent are all things that are composed.

2.5.2.2 The lesson has special application to man. The methods of Buddhist meditation urge one to meditate on old age, on sickness, on death. To concentrate on death, and to make it more real in anticipation, men are advised to go, either in imagination or in fact, to places of cremation, in order to contemplate the decomposing bodies and half-consumed bones.

So far we have considered only one aspect of the cosmic illusion (māyā) and of the need to undeceive oneself.

2.5.2.3 *Sabbe dhammā anatta.* All the constituent elements of beings—those elements whose presence together is taken to constitute substance—are in reality *insubstantial*. They are temporary agglomerations without substance. By a sort of atomic theory, Buddhism invites us to divide mentally every apparently solid substance into smaller and smaller 'fragments', which finally become so small that they have no longer any extension or any duration, and which die in the very moment in which they appear to be replaced by others. It is a theory which could be compared, in modern terms, with the illusion of a continuous image which television provides for us by means of discontinuous points, ceaselessly appearing and disappearing. What has just been said about the insubstantiality of all things is a universal principle, of which we have already considered the particular application to the insubstantiality and 'not-self' of man. (Refer back to §2.4.3 and to *Reader*, §3.2.5 'There is no ego'.) Thus, as one text puts it:

> There is no agent, one finds only action.
> A way exists, but there is no wayfarer.
> (Visuddhi-Magga, XVI)

2.5.2.4 The same text brings us to the heart of the problem, and to the third dramatic characteristic of human existence when it adds:

> 'There is no one who is miserable, but misery truly exists.'

*Sorrow* is the third essential characteristic of man. It is because the Buddha was profoundly impressed by it that he discovered and put forward his doctrine. He is the physician who seeks to treat human sorrow, according to a comparison which he himself employed. Sorrow is the natural consequence of the two preceding characteristics (§§2.5.2.1 and 2.5.2.3), for these two realities contradict the whole of our natural aspirations. How wretched is man if, as the Buddha declares in his first and most important sermon, the sermon of Benares, the deepest meaning of sorrow is 'to be subject to what one does not love, and separated from what one loves'. He would like to be solid and substantial, and he finds that he is brittle and insubstantial; he would like to be everlasting, and he finds that he is embroiled in an endless series of births, each of which leads him to one more death. An endless process of beginning again is without doubt the greatest of sorrows, for it is the deprivation of peace. Peace is ordered stability.

### 2.5.2.5 Exercise

I now suggest two exercises to summarize what we have been discussing in the preceding paragraphs:

(a) First read *Reader* §§3.1.5 'The sermon on burning', and 3.2.4 'Fruitful and barren karma'. Refer again to the first part of 'The Benares Sermon' (*Reader*, §3.1.4); and consult also, 'The Struggle for Freedom', *Encyclopedia*, pp. 282–4. Then write your comments on this passage from the Sermon on Burning:

> Everything is burning.... And with what fire is it burning?... With the fire of lust, with the fire of anger, with the fire of ignorance ... with birth, decay, death, grief, lamentation, suffering, dejection and despair.

(b) Secondly, give a fuller explanation, according to Buddhist teaching, of this further text: 'The King of death cannot touch him who looks upon the world as a mirage'.

### PLEASE PAUSE HERE
DO NOT READ ON UNTIL YOU HAVE COMPLETED THE EXERCISE

### 2.5.2.6 Specimen answer

(a) 'Fire' is all that torments and consumes man. This fire burns at three different levels:

(i)   The *experience* of the precariousness of human life, which is expressed here in three words—birth (which is rebirth, endless rebirth, according to the karma doctrine); decay or old age (which, in those times, came very soon); and death. Meditation on death has always been regarded in Buddhism as an important means towards enlightenment.

(ii)  The *feelings* men have when they think of their own insecurity and impermanence: misery and sorrow, grief and lamentation, despair.

(iii) The origin of this despair is in the *belief* that things are real and really affect us.

Men are 'burning' with three fundamental passions: with covetousness for what they like; with hatred for what they fear; and with ignorance and foolishness, which makes them think phenomena are real—whereas they are impermanent and without substance, and are themselves part of the vale of sorrow.

Finally, as the Buddha declared in the Benares Sermon, the empire of sorrow comes from the desire we have for objects and for our own personality. Only suppression of desire will extinguish the fire of suffering. The idea of sorrow being born from attachment to or desire for material realities is found also in Hinduism, but it has not the same central role there that it has in Buddhism.

(b) We may hope to pass beyond the reach of harm and evil by freeing ourselves of the basic illusions about the world. The world is a mirage because:

(i)   although it is impermanent, men take it as permanent (see §§2.5.2.1 above);

(ii)  although it is without any solid substance or existence, men take it as a substantial reality (see §§2.5.2.3 above);

(iii) although it is sorrowful, men try vainly to find in it their happiness (see §§2.5.2.4 above);

When we realize that the world is a mirage, we do not incur the consequences of ignorance, which are death followed by a sorrowful rebirth. (The 'King of death' is Māra, a kind of 'Buddhist Satan'.)

## 2.6  The path to deliverance

### 2.6.1  The middle way

2.6.1.1 How then can one escape from this wheel of rebirths? In the last analysis, it is the only thing which Buddhism claims to teach, a claim repeated, using various expressions, in a hundred different texts.

2.6.1.2 First it is to be said that it is not by the desperate act of *suicide* that one can escape. This culpable and ill-advised act inevitability throws one into a still more sorrowful rebirth. The Buddha himself advised against it, even if certain of his disciples have sometimes dallied with the idea of suicide or even had recourse to it.

2.6.1.3 Nor is the path by way of ascetical practices, however excruciating, as certain contemporary teachers used to recommend in his time. The Buddha did try them himself; among other austerities he undertook long and strict fasts, which almost cost him his life. After his experience of these methods, he affirmed that they led to nothing except a slower suicide, and one which was just as inefficacious as the more sudden forms of suicide.

2.6.1.4 Nor, it appears, can one gain final deliverance by *prayer*, that is by having recourse to the help of supernatural beings. From the time that he left his family circle with its classical rituals of prayer, the Buddha abandoned them and declared that they were without ultimate value or efficacy. Despite the popular belief in the gods and in their power, he says, they cannot help men. Rather, they are themselves subject to the three ills which afflict man, and they too need to be liberated from them. If they are to escape from rebirths, all, from the demons right up to the supreme deva Brahmā, must listen to the doctrine of the Buddha and must adopt his 'middle way', which holds 'the mean between an excess of pleasure and an excess of austerity'. It would be relevant to read here *Reader*, §3.2.6 'Two kinds of quest', and to refer again to *Reader*, §§3.2.7 'Good conduct', and 3.3.2 'The Ten Precepts'.

### 2.6.2  The principle of the path

2.6.2.1 But what then, seen from a positive point of view, is this path which the Buddha proposes, and of which he himself says that it is 'difficult to understand, and difficult to follow', and that many will not adopt it?

2.6.2.2 He himself, and following him all the Buddhist texts and schools, have given diverse descriptions of this path. It would be an unduly long and complicated task to try to examine the many relevant texts in detail here. The basic principle of them all is: One must kill all desire, for it is always from unsatisfied desire that sorrow is born, and the endless rebirths are themselves caused by actions which desire has provoked. But desire is rooted in our illusions; so the illusions must be destroyed. How is this to be achieved?

## 2.7 The noble disciple

### 2.7.1 Notions of good and evil

Before we speak of the precise forms that the struggle takes, we should note that the notions of good and of evil which are familiar in other traditions (such as conformity to or rebellion against the will of God, in the Christian tradition, or reference to some other supreme sanction in other religions) do not exist in the same way in the moral thought-world of Buddhism.

### 2.7.2 Right views

Ideas are not accepted because a light from on high has communicated them to men with divine authority; but only if they are in themselves just and exact (*samma*). They are not rejected because of the prohibition of some exterior power, but because they are seen to be false (*miccha*). It is only in the Mahāyāna branch of Buddhism, and then only for unsophisticated disciples who still have temporary need of such beliefs, that truths are presented as things to be believed on the word of the Master, without needing to be criticized further and to be personally assimilated.

Of all the 'right views', the most central and the most important is to recognize that nothing is even capable of arousing desire if one looks at it aright. The Japanese Buddhist poets of the Middle Ages said this repeatedly in their verses (*haikai*): The life of man is like the wake of a ship in the sea; scarcely has it been traced before it disappears.... All reality is like the fragile blossom of the pink cherry-tree; it opens in the morning and is already withered in the chill of the evening...

### 2.7.3 Right actions

2.7.3.1 Actions should not be undertaken because some divine authority has ordered them, but only because they are useful for personal liberation (*kusala*). They are avoided only because they are useless for that purpose (*akusala*). The great 'right action' is to abandon the world, relinquishing all objects in order to cause desire for them to cease; thus one procures for oneself the leisure to meditate at length on the great 'right notion' which has just been described, in §2.7.2. (Here refer again to *Reader*. §§3.1.1 'The Great Retirement' and 3.2.8 'Show me an island'.)

2.7.3.2 So it is that the monk, for whom the layfolk out of respect guarantee the necessities of life by providing food and shelter, marches freely towards the ultimate goal. And the fundamental ambition of the layman ought to be to become a monk himself, in this life or at least in a subsequent life. Here read *Reader*, §§3.3.3 'Four fundamental attitudes of a noble disciple'; 3.3.4 'The wise and thoughtful Bikkhu' (i.e. monk); and 3.4.3 'The four Spiritual Dwellings'. On the monastic ideal, and the stages of discipleship, read the section entitled '*Sangha*' in Horner's article (*Encyclopedia*, pp. 290–2).

### 2.7.3.3 Exercise

There is an ancient canonical text, which claims to give a summary of the whole destiny of man: 'Cease to do evil, learn to do good, cleanse your own heart'. In the light of the foregoing paragraphs, say how each of these precepts should be understood. For this exercise, refer also to the *Reader*, §3.2.7 'Good Conduct' and 3.3.2 'The Ten Precepts'

**PLEASE PAUSE HERE**

DO NOT READ ON UNTIL YOU HAVE COMPLETED THE EXERCISE

### 2.7.3.4 Specimen answer and discussion

The rule may be said to apply, in a general sense, to all religions. But it takes a special meaning according to the tenets of Buddhism.

*'Cease to do evil'* will mean observe the five great Precepts—or, if a monk, other Precepts in addition (see *Reader*, §3.3.2).

*'Learn to do good'* means, for laymen hear the doctrine, give alms to the monks, and finally become a monk yourself, in order to attain to fuller spiritual liberation. For monks it means study, preach, meditate on the doctrine.

*'Cleanse your heart'* means eliminate the 'evil' thoughts, those false views which do not lead to liberation (cf. §2.7.2 above): and avoid 'evil' actions (§2.7.3 above). A 'pure' heart knows that nothing existing is worth desiring, that by eradication of all desires, and by right meditation, one will reach liberation. And the man who has such a pure heart, acts accordingly.

## 2.8   The great achievement

### 2.8.1  Achievement—not grace

Taking the viewpoint of orthodox classical Buddhism, it is indeed man's 'achievement' with which we are concerned and not 'grace' or supernatural help. In fact the monk, although he be illuminated by the example and the counsels of the Founder, cannot ultimately depend on anyone or anything else except himself, in order to arrive at his goal. The 'Last instructions of the Buddha' (*Reader*, §3.1.7) are explicit on this point. Study here the section on 'The Aryan Eightfold Path' in the *Encyclopedia*, pp. 284–8.

### 2.8.2  Nirvāna

2.8.2.1 We have no space here to trace in detail the process by which a man who was formerly shackled to many material objects and troubled by many desires, progressively detaches himself from them when he becomes a monk. He sweeps far away from himself worldly goods, political intrigues and the pride of intellectual research. He empties his spirit of complicated thoughts, then proceeds to empty it of the simpler thoughts and eventually of any trace of all thought. So at last he arrives at an ineffable state which is 'neither awareness nor absence of awareness'. He comes as if to a place of refuge, an island, a state of immortality, which is called Nirvāna.

2.8.2.2 On Nirvāna (or Nibbāna) read the following sections in the *Reader*, §§3.1.2 'Enjoying the bliss of emancipation'; 3.4.4 'The Way to the highest meditations'; 3.5.2 'Emptiness'; and 3.5.4 'Nāgārjuna: No difference between Samsāra and Nirvāna'. Read also *Ling*, §§2.3.5–2.3.7 and *Encyclopedia*, pp. 288–90. (In §2.9.3ff. below we shall be saying something more about the questions which the doctrine of Nirvāna raises, especially in the minds of Western commentators.)

### 2.8.2.3 Exercise

After reading the passages I have just indicated, try to set down your own understanding of what you take Nirvāna to mean. You could do so by writing a commentary on the following lines, written by Edwin Arnold.

> If any teach Nirvāna is 'to cease', say unto such: they lie,
> If any teach Nirvāna is 'to live' say unto such: they err,
> Not knowing 'this', nor what light shines beyond their broken lamps,
> Nor lifeless, timeless bliss.

PLEASE PAUSE HERE

DO NOT READ ON UNTIL YOU HAVE COMPLETED THE EXERCISE

### 2.8.2.4 Specimen answer

One might paraphrase the author's lines as follows:

Nirvāna, being an experiential, 'trans-rational' situation, cannot be precisely expressed. In this realm of the inexpressible, words are unavailing. To say that Nirvāna is 'to cease', is a lie first because this man has never really existed (cf. §2.5.2.2); and to say that it is 'to live' is an error, because this man does not really live as a permanent entity. Secondly, and at a deeper level, it is false to say that Nirvāna is 'to cease', because it is positive fulfilment, not simply annihilation; and it is an error to say it is 'to live', because 'living' implies the kind of individual existence experienced in the round of samsāra—and that no longer applies in the plenitude of Nirvāna. The 'lamp' of the ordinary knowledge is useless here; it has to be abandoned, 'broken'. The 'light' of the Nirvāna experience is 'beyond'; it can only be pointed to as 'this'. And one who has achieved the experience knows that it liberates from all desires and sorrows; he knows it is 'bliss'.

## 2.9 Problems and queries

### 2.9.1 The destiny of man

In every age man raises questions about his destiny. The Buddha was not a philosopher nor a speculative religious thinker. He refused to give any reply to questions which seem, to Westerners in particular, so fundamental, such as the questions of the eternity or the non-eternity of the world, of the survival or the annihilation of the soul after death. To answer either Yes or No seemed to him as both equally dangerous and equally useless for the cure of man's ills, as he proposed it, and indeed apt to distract attention from it. Recall the account of the Buddha's lengthy refusal to discuss such matters, in *Reader*, §3.4.5 'Questions which do not help spiritual progress'.

### 2.9.1.1 Exercise

It is sometimes said that Buddhists were 'the first rationalists'. Discuss the meaning of this term, and ask whether it is rightly applied in this connection. Before writing your comments, look at *Reader*, §3.5.2 'Emptiness'.

PLEASE PAUSE HERE

DO NOT READ ON UNTIL YOU HAVE COMPLETED THE EXERCISE

### 2.9.6.2 Specimen answer and discussion

The word 'rationalist' is ambiguous. In its more usual meaning, it implies that one relies *only* on the power of human reason, and that one rejects any other source of knowledge, such as faith or divine revelation. Apart from this primary meaning, the word may also imply that one relies on the power of reason to arrive at the greatest fulfilment of which the human mind is capable. Buddhists are 'rationalists' in the primary sense of the word, inasmuch as they reject any external religious authority claiming to communicate truth to them from divine revelation. Each one must arrive at the truth by his own mental effort. As regards asserting the ultimate power of human reason, Buddhists differ from Western rationalists in their estimate of the mind's capabilities. In the first stages of their meditation, indeed, they do use reason to hear, to consider and to accept the essential Noble Truths of Buddhist doctrine. However, the more a Buddhist is progressing on the path to liberation, the more he has to abandon all the useless problems and futile solutions of the reasoning mind. He must reject the ordinary paths of mental activity and arrive at an 'emptiness' of all thought, in which lies his mysterious liberation.

### 2.9.2  The social question

The first difficulty which some modern Western inquirers may put to the Buddhist who is in process of liberating himself, is that his path seems to be ego-centred and negative. What part does the world itself play in this journey? What service does the individual monk render to the world of men in their countless millions? This is what might be called the 'social objection'. (Max Weber, indeed, describes Buddhism as 'a-social', as Ling notes on page 95 of your set-book.) For a long time Buddhism has seemed vulnerable to this objection, at least in the life of its monks. Monks are recommended to have only dispassionate 'sentiments' of benevolence and compassion towards the rest of men. It is the Buddhist laymen who, at various times, have proceeded to practical philanthropy. Like the Indian king Aśoka, they concerned themselves with stopping wars among their peoples, with doing good to the destitute, to travellers, to pilgrims, and to all spiritual men.

What Buddhism in its classical form has offered men is essentially the 'gift of the Dhamma', either in preaching or in a general teaching which has given rise to schools and universities. The 'social motivation' of the Buddha's teaching is emphasized in the passage quoted in the *Reader*, §3.1.3 'The Buddha hesitates to preach'. *Ling*, §§2.38–2.39 puts forward some stimulating reflections on the sociological significance of the Buddhist Sangha. *Ling*, §6.44 provides an answer to the objection of Max Weber, who assumed that a social ethic has no place in Buddhism.

### 2.9.3  The question of Nirvāna

2.9.3.1 This question has been the theme of endless discussions in Europe. Some scholars, such as the Russian Stcherbatsky, have seen Nirvāna as something negative; others, like de la Vallée-Poussin, have on the other hand presented it as something positive. Both schools find support for their views in the Buddhist texts which sometimes underline one aspect, sometimes the other. But what all the texts declare, as do the living Buddhists whom one may consult, is that 'The one who has entered Nirvāna does not exist, but Nirvāna exists, (Visuddhi-Magga, XVIII).

2.9.3.2 This cryptic phrase points to two preoccupations of Buddhism which are apparently difficult to reconcile, and which are reflected in the lines of Edwin Arnold, quoted above in §2.8.2.2. On the one hand, it is necessary to root out completely the idea of personal identity, for to admit it would be to sow infallibly the seeds of desire. There has never been, there is not, there never will be a *self*. There is no 'I'. On the other hand, who is not sensitive to the yearning cry, deep in man and in all being, to be and to remain to the end some positive reality? Even though this ultimate end may remain unexplained and inexplicable, the human heart longs for some *happiness* in it.

2.9.3.3 So some commentators accuse Buddhism of incoherence and of contradiction in its doctrine on the destiny of man. Others, and the Buddhists themselves, reply that one must inevitably realize that this situation reflects the fundamental problem of man himself, who has to go beyond himself in order to achieve what he is—even to the point of losing himself. And what is it to lose oneself? To such questions the Founder would certainly have refused to reply. He would have said:

> My whole message has only one taste—deliverance...
> Work out your salvation with all diligence.

### 2.9.3.4 Exercise
To recapitulate the points made in this section (the whole of §2), write down a brief summary of *how* one is to attain to liberation, according to classical Buddhist teaching.

### PLEASE PAUSE HERE
DO NOT READ ON UNTIL YOU HAVE COMPLETED THE EXERCISE

### 2.9.3.5 Specimen answer
Buddhist liberation can only come from one's own efforts (§2.8.1). One should not undertake extraordinary ascetical practices (§2.6.1.3), nor rely on prayers to any deity (§2.6.1.4); but one must liberate oneself from error and folly by following the Noble Eightfold Path (see the Benares Sermon and *Encyclopedia*, pp 284–5), which leads to the highest meditations and to Nirvāna (see *Reader*, §3.4.4).

The Buddha Gautama (and other Buddhas in other periods) point the way, by preaching the Noble Truths and showing how to discern 'right views', 'right actions', and 'right meditations'. But Buddhas do not 'help', nor can they help. It is for each individual to do his own ploughing, 'looking not for refuge to anyone besides himself'. Each one must abandon what the world holds dear, observe the precepts, and meditate upon the truth, in order to arrive at Nirvāna.

# 3 DEVELOPMENTS OF BUDDHISM

Earlier we described the essential internal problem with which Buddhism is preoccupied: the universal phenomenon of suffering and the method advocated for its elimination, which is the eradication of desire.

But Buddhism is also a living reality which has existed for 2,500 years. It is now necessary to outline the vicissitudes, both doctrinal and structural, to which Buddhism's Teaching (Dhamma) and its Order (Sangha) have been subject.

This long history will be related within two perspectives. First, that of geographical expansion, together with the cultural encounters to which this has given rise. All religious and social systems are influenced by environment and events. Secondly, that of doctrinal and institutional development. A religion does not submit passively to outside influences, but reacts to new elements that it encounters when it enters new regions.

The result of these exchanges has always meant for Buddhism the acquisition of new features, and enrichment of many of its doctrines and institutions. Often this has led to changes in the original forms of Buddhism, under pressure from ideas and influences very different from it in nature, and even hostile to it.

## 3.1 The geographical spread of Buddhism

### 3.1.1 In India itself

Buddhism existed in India for more than 1000 years before its virtual disappearance. Naturally such a long history was not uneventful.

3.1.1.1 During the period of the Buddha's own preaching (c. 520–480 BC.) Buddhism seems to have spread chiefly in North-East India—in the native country of the Founder, the Magadha, and in the surrounding kingdoms. In spite of these early successes, the Buddhist 'sect' was just one among many; it remained so for some time.

Buddhism appealed to all castes; all were equally welcomed—an innovation at that time. It seems however that the upper classes were at first better represented. The Buddha himself was of the second caste, of nobles and warriors. Many of his disciples were members of the brahmanic or ruling castes. Nevertheless, more than once, he said that virtue, and not birth, made a man 'spiritual', made him 'brāhman'. The brāhmans, proud of their religious and social position and of their monopoly of ritual functions, were difficult to win over; the nobles, *kshatriyas*, were easier, even enthusiastic converts. There were, as well, a considerable number of disciples of lowly origin. Ānanda, for whom the Buddha had a great affection, was of very humble origin.

3.1.1.2 **Three** factors contributed to the development of the distinctive characteristics of Indian Buddhism. The **first**, an internal factor, was the development of a *plurality of schools* of different ways of thought and 'spirituality'. Here, as everywhere when a religious doctrine is propagated, there were two main types of believer. The 'Ancients', called *Sthavira* or *Thera*, were strict conservatives; the traditions they preserved are still kept today in the Canon of Scriptures written later in the Pali language—a language close to Maghadhī, the language of the Founder. This 'ancient' tradition was considered to be more authentic and pure—by its followers at least. The innovators, who called themselves 'Members of the Great Assembly' (*Mahāsanghikas*), seem to have been less bound by tradition. At any rate they recorded in Sanskrit (a more 'scholarly' language than Pali) a doctrine which was more open to further development, in which the influence of the Buddhist laity (as distinct from the monks) was especially significant. It is from them that the form of Buddhism which is called 'the Greater Vehicle' (Mahāyāna) was to emerge. Each of these two bodies of opinion was later to become dominant and formative in its own particular geographical areas. The article by Horner in the *Encyclopedia* (pp. 263–92) relates chiefly to the doctrines and practices of Theravada Buddhism. A treatment of the special perspectives of Mahāyāna Buddhism is given in the article by Edward Conze in the *Encyclopedia* (pp. 293–317).

### 3.1.1.3 Exercise

Two names have been commonly given to the Buddhism of South and South East Asia: Theravāda and Hīnayāna. Refer to §1.3.2.2 above and to the Glossary, to the explanations of the terms in the *Encyclopedia*, pp. 264–5 and p. 293; and to *Ling*, §§4.30–1; then write your own brief explanation of the meaning and origin of both names. You will also meet the name 'Theravādins'. Does this simply mean the same as 'followers of the Theravāda school? Also, in your answer, say where Theravādin Buddhism is dominant today.

PLEASE PAUSE HERE

DO NOT READ ON UNTIL YOU HAVE COMPLETED THE EXERCISE

### 3.1.1.4 Specimen answer

During the first period of Buddhism, the 'conservative school', which as we have seen, was called Thera or Sthavira, claimed to possess the authentic teachings of the Founder in their tradition, enshrined in what was to become the Pali Canon. But the more 'progressive' monks and laymen claimed to have a broader mind and a more complete tradition; contemptuously they called the ancient tradition a Hīnayāna, that is: a small, narrow, low way, or 'vehicle'; and they called themselves the Mahāyāna—the Great Way. 'Theravādins' is a name more specifically given to one of the eighteen sects of the Hīnayāna in antiquity. All the other seventeen disappeared centuries ago when Buddhism was submerged in Northern India. The Theravādins are dominant in the Southern area of Buddhist Asia, and theirs is the national religion in Sri Lanka, Burma and Thailand. I shall say more about these two 'vehicles' in §3.2 below.

---

3.1.1.5 This tension between rival opinions, and the growing divergence between different schools, led to efforts to re-establish 'pure' doctrine. This in turn gave rise to the **second** important factor in the situation after the death of the Master: that is, the calling together of *Councils*, intended to establish the essential content of the sacred texts and the principal disciplinary rules.

3.1.1.6 The history of these Councils is surrounded by legends; the First

Council (held at Rajgir—see §1.3.2.1 above, and *Encyclopedia*, p. 264) took place immediately after the death of the Founder and is held to have determined the doctrinal and disciplinary body (dharmavinaya); the Second Council (see §1.3.2.2 above, and *Encyclopedia*, pp. 264–5) and the Third Council tried to tackle the problem of doctrinal dissensions. It was the Fourth Council that sanctioned the split between the 'Lesser Vehicle' (Hīnayana) of the Ancients and the 'Greater Vehicle' (Mahāyāna). Other Theravāda Councils were held in later times. In the calling and conduct of Councils, Buddhists do not admit a supreme authority. The Councils were, and are, an initiative of local, national, or world federations of Buddhists.

3.1.1.7 It was at the time of the Third Council that the **third** determining factor in the development of Buddhism in India emerged: namely, the conversion to Buddhism of Aśoka, a powerful monarch of northern and central India. (See *Ling*, §3.26). Aśoka was officially greeted with the title '*Piyadasi*', meaning 'of benign contenance'. In reality he hardly deserved this epithet before his conversion, involved as he was with bloody campaigns; but once converted he became worthy of it. He ordered to be inscribed on pillars or on rock faces in many places 'Edicts' enjoining observance of 'the

*Figure 15 Lauriya Nandangarh (Bihar) edict pillar erected by King Aśoka, Mauryan c.242–241 BC. (Reproduced by permission of the Director of the India Office Library and Records.)*

Law'. In reality, these Edicts were neither specifically nor exclusively Buddhist; they enjoined the classical virtues within the Indian religious tradition: non-violence, tolerance, benevolence, and charity. (see *Reader*, §3.4.7 'Aśoka's Rock Edict', for the text of Edict XIII). The ruler's piety was beneficial to Buddhism and also to other groups during his reign of 40 years from 272–232 BC (see *Ling*, §3.27).

3.1.1.8 In Christian history, the emperor Constantine was very important because he not only gave toleration to Christianity in the fourth century CE, but he and his successors went on to make Christianity the official religion of the Roman Empire. Can you suggest a brief comparison and contrast between those Christian Roman Emperors and Aśoka?

---

*Brief answer*: There is this similarity, that both Constantine and Aśoka underwent a religious conversion, and proclaimed their esteem for a 'new' religion. However those Christian Roman Emperors were exclusive in their zeal for Christianity, and they banned pagan cults; Aśoka, even if very sympathetic to Buddhism, never banned other religions. Rather, he proclaimed the general principles of natural and traditional ethics which Buddhism had received from the past.

3.1.1.9 Thus began 1000 years of prosperity, then of decadence for Buddhism in India. Between the second and the sixth centuries CE, the schools of philosophy produced their greatest masters: Buddhagosa, Vasubandhu, Nāgārjuna, Asanga. Buddhist universities flourished, such as Nālanda. Pilgrims, such as the Chinese Fa-Hien and Hiuen-Tsang, came to visit the Holy Places. The faithful were strong in number.

3.1.1.10 After the Fourth Council the two main streams in Buddhism's spiritual quest became more and more clearly distinguished—particularly in their attitude towards the Founder. In Theravāda, man's quest can rely only on its own resources, according to the last instruction of the dying Buddha: 'Be to yourself your own lamp, your own refuge'. The Buddha is in this religious outlook only a master and example, vanished from the world and inactive. In Mahāyāna, he becomes a mysterious being, who continues to radiate light and strength towards men, and whose ashes are worthy of a cult in tomb-shrines (*stupas*); temples contain his statues and sculptures tell his story, which is embellished by many legendary tales. As time went on, many Buddhists, especially the pious layfolk, came to look confidently to the Buddha for protection.

3.1.1.11 However in India, Hinduism, with its gods, with its masses of faithful adherents, with its priests carrying out its many forms of public cult, and with its pilgrimages and sacrifices, remained all-pervasive and very strong in its hold on the allegiance of the people. It was this Hinduism, given official support in later times, that (from about the eleventh century CE) re-engulfed Indian Buddhism—which had in any case become overlaid by popular superstitions. After the Muslim conquest of North India Buddhism disappeared from the land of its origin, with the exception of the Holy Places connected with the birth, the enlightenment, the first sermon and the death of the Buddha; and with the exception, also, of the Northern Himalyan frontier. (See *Ling*, §6.41; note there the various reasons which have been suggested to explain the extinction of Buddhism in India.)

47

### 3.1.2 Expansion outside India

3.1.2.1 What Buddhism lost in India, it more than recouped outside it. The Indian peninsula offered the Buddhists two main routes to the outside world. One was the link by sea to the South and East; the other was by land over the mountains to the North and again to the East. The spread of Buddhism towards the West was to remain limited to the frontier regions, between India, Afghanistan and the countries to a greater or lesser extent hellenized by Alexander the Great and his successors. Among these Indo-Greek kingdoms was that of a king Milinda (Menandros or Menander), whose dialogues with the Buddhists in his domains are a classic work: *Questions of King Milinda (Milindapañha)*. Often these are penetrating, even caustic, questions, fairly representative of the inquisitive and argumentative mind of the Greek tradition.

3.1.2.2 **The Southern route** was by sea, leading to the islands and peninsulas of South and South-East Asia. Among the countries reached by this route are the following:

*Sri Lanka (Ceylon)*. According to legend, Buddhism was brought there by Aśoka's son, Mahinda, who himself became a monk and attained Nirvāna. It was also in Sri Lanka that the Pāli Canon of the Ancients is said to have been preserved by recitation of the sacred Scriptures, and definitely fixed. The old Buddhist chronicles of the island show the increasing influence of Buddhism on all social classes and on all aspects of life. Account was also taken of the needs of popular devotion in rituals, some of them of an almost magical nature—such as *pirit*, an incantation of texts against demons. Local Buddhist Councils were held in Sri Lanka and large impressive structures were built, as at Anuradhapura and Kandy. Ceylon is one of the countries where the Community, the Sangha, still appears to be very much alive: as witness the monasteries, the universities, the publication of books and reviews, and also the great popular festivals. A famous example of the latter is to be seen in the processions from the temple of the Buddha's Tooth. (For further details of the progress of Buddhism in Ceylon, read *Ling*, §§4.38 and 6.43–5.)

3.1.2.3 *Burma*. The emperor Aśoka is believed to have sent missionaries there about 250 BC. There followed a long period during which Buddhism co-existed with Hinduism and popular superstitions. Finally Buddhism emerged as the official religion of the country, to such an extent that Burmese monasticism and sanctuaries still have a powerful attraction for many Buddhists, including pilgrims from abroad. Like Sri Lanka, Burma is a land of Theravāda Buddhism. (For the origins and development of Burmese Buddhism refer to *Ling*, §§5.27, 6.42, 6.43 and 6.46.)

Buddhism in *Thailand* has the same characteristics as in Burma.

3.1.2.4 The *Peninsula of Indochina*, has, because of its position, been submitted to the influence of Theravāda from the South and of Mahāyāna from the North. Its Buddhism is thus far more 'mixed'. It is in fact widely influenced not only by the animist beliefs of the mountain people (to some extent a similar factor was also operative in the case of the other countries discussed above) but also by the religious examples of nearby China, with its immense prestige as a civilizing force. In *Indochina* is to be found one of the most beautiful Buddhist temples, Angkor Wat. As I noted earlier, its superimposed terraces are designed to offer an image of the world, at the same time as being 'spiritually' uplifting. In *Indonesia*, and especially in *Java*, the influence of Buddhism was of great importance for 1000 years, until the arrival of Islam. The temple of Borobudur remains as a magnificent reminder of this period.

*Figure 16 Capital of Lion column and edict of King Aśoka excavated at Sarnath, near Benares. (Mansell Collection.)*

*Figure 17 Presenting food to the monks at New Year Ceremony, Thailand. (Information Service of Thailand, London.)*

3.1.2.5 **The Nortern route** went via the high desert plateaux of Central Asia; it followed the same paths taken by nomadic nations, military expeditions and commercial caravans. In the spread of Buddhism, this route, and especially the silk route to China, has been used primarily (but not exclusively) by the Mahāyāna. Some Central Asian towns, used as staging posts, thus acquired considerable importance in the dissemination of Buddhism, and many valuable texts have been found at these places, for instance at Loyang.

3.1.2.6 Undoubtedly the most decisive success of expanding Buddhism took place in *China*, which was then the cultural and political power towards which all the surrounding countries looked for example and authority. You have a fuller treatment of the development and later history of Buddhism in China in the article by R. H. Robinson, 'Buddhism: in China and Japan', in the *Encyclopedia*, pp. 318–37; refer also to *Ling*, §§4.36, 4.37, 5.20–5.23 and 6.47.

3.1.2.7 From the first century CE there were Buddhists in Kiangsu; in the middle of the second century the Emperor Han was converted. About this time an 'office of translations' was created for the sacred texts which were mostly in Sanskrit and Chinese. The fidelity of the translators was remarkable: today it is possible to reconstruct, almost literally, a lost Sanskrit original from such a translation. The activity of these translators was prolific, and covered some thousands of long and short treatises.

3.1.2.8 In practice, Buddhism in China was remarkably accommodating. It followed the bent of the Chinese mind, which had always been practical, moralistic, not very doctrinaire, anxious to keep the peace in social relations and tolerant of diverse opinions. Later I shall be saying something about two distinctive religious trends which emerged in China. One led to transcendental meditation (the T'ien T'ai sect); the other to the devotion and invocation of certain Buddhas who were believed to be able to bestow aid on their devotees (e.g. as in the Amida cult).

3.1.2.9 Towards the sixth and seventh centuries CE Chinese Buddhism began to develop deeper doctrinal roots. More and more pilgrims went to India; they brought back texts—either canonical Scriptures or works of later schools—for careful translation. This material gave rise to a great deal of discussion and reflection. Increasingly, from this time onwards, Buddhism became one of the three religions of China, together with Confucianism and Taoism. There is an tolerant, syncretistic maxim, which well sums up the accommodating attitude of the Chinese: 'The *three* religions are *one* religion'.

3.1.2.10 As one would expect, popular devotion gave rise to many accretions of rites, observances and superstitions. Everywhere in the temples there were statues of Buddhas—Buddhas in the plural, for it was believed that each age had its own Buddhas. The walls were covered by paintings of heavens and hells, depicted in many different forms. Pilgrimages to sacred mountains; visits to cemeteries where monks kept guard over the ashes of the ancestors; rosaries with 108 beads, untiringly fingered to mark the recitation of praises of the Founder; the invocation by both laity and monks of the name of Amida, 'Namo-O-mi-to-fu'—all these were features of Buddhism in the tolerant climate of China.

3.1.2.11 It was this syncretistic Chinese Buddhism which made its way into *Korea*, where once again it merged with the local religion, resulting in a mixture of four components. However, under the aegis of certain rulers, vassals of China who were deeply influenced by the strong Buddhist element in Chinese culture at this time, Buddhism held a very important position. So

it came about that Korea served as a bridge for the passage of Buddhism into Japan.

3.1.2.12 Buddhism entered *Japan* in the sixth century CE. (You have material for the study of the progress of Japanese Buddhism in pp. 337–41 of Robinson's article in the *Encyclopedia*; and in *Ling*, §§5.24. 5.28, 6.48 and 7.43.) The country was still divided into feudal clans and culturally backward. Introduced into the country by Korean scholars, Buddhism was regarded as the 'modern doctrine' by Japanese progressives. They used it as a weapon against Shinto, the traditional religion which was the belief and inspiration of the conservative guardians of the feudal order. (In this course we do not have a separate treatment of Shinto, but you are recommended, if you have time, to read the fifteen-page article on that subject by G. Bownas, 'Shinto', in the *Encyclopedia*, pp. 342—56). About 600 CE, the devout regent Shōtoku, the son of Buddhist parents, took the side of the Soga clan, which was progressive in its ideas and had embraced Buddhism. According to the custom of the time, it was taken for granted that the people followed their masters in religious allegiance.

3.1.2.13 Twelve sects were to emerge. Each of these sought to be distinctive but within almost all of them there were further divisions and, moreover, there was often interaction between one sect and another. Alliances were established, in a spirit of compromise, with Shinto. Thus some buildings were intended to be used partly as Buddhist temples and partly as Shinto temples. Shinto divinities were sometimes represented as avatars of the Buddha.

3.1.2.14 By a decree of the regent Shōtoku, Buddhism became the State religion of Japan. The result, during the following centuries, was a mingling of monastery and court, of the spiritual and the worldly. High dignitaries, following the Indian and Chinese example, sometimes became monks; monks directed the conscience and the policies of those who held office. Some monasteries, like that on Mount Hiei overlooking Kyōto, controlled vast estates and had thousands of dependants. They sometimes became so troublesome that the regents of the empire (*shōgun*) had to wage war against them to break their power. Besides the monks, the monasteries housed administrators, builders, poets, artists, and even military tacticians. Gradually Buddhism spread outwards from the court and the aristocracy to become the religion of the people.

3.1.2.15 Buddhism remained the State religion until 1860, when Japan's entry into the modern world coincided with a new awareness of national identity and a return to the national cult of Shinto. After the re-establishment of Shinto it nevertheless remained a very important landowner, until the recent agrarian reforms sponsored by the American occupying forces after the last war. I shall be returning to the fortunes of Buddhism in China and Japan in the present century, in §§4.3 and 4.4 below.

(a)

(b)

Figure 19 It has been suggested that the pagoda evolved from the stupa: (a) Great Stupa at Sanchi. (Mansell Collection); (b) Ruanveliseya temple, Arunadhapura, Ceylon. (J. Allan Cash.); (c) Wat Phra Tadt Harinpoonchai (Royal Monastery) in Lampoon, northern Thailand. (Information Service of Thailand, London.); (d) Horuji temple and pagoda, Nara, Japan. (Popperfoto.)

(c)

(d)

3.1.2.16 It was also by the Northern route (by way of China as well as North Eastern India) that Buddhism finally took possession of *Tibet*. Here it developed in a completely distinctive way, a mixture of old superstitions with the new religion, leading to original and subtle developments of spiritual doctrines and practices. In this process Tibet eventually became a monastery kingdom.

Now, to recall the salient points in this brief geographical and historical survey, jot down the names of countries in which Buddhism became a *State* religion.

---

*An answer*: In almost all the countries mentioned above, Buddhism was officially adopted by the rulers at one time or another. This development was most clearly seen in the Buddhism of the South—Sri Lanka, Thailand, Burma, and also in Japan in certain periods. The situation was more complex in China, where Confucianism remained a dominating influence in Chinese life; and also in Tibet, where pre-existing local practices and attitudes considerably modified the form which Buddhism took as the State religion.

### 3.1.3  Buddhist missionaries and their methods

3.1.3.1 By whom and how was Buddhism spread throughout the East? From what you have read so far, probably you are already able to answer these questions. The **bearers** of the message were travellers, fervent exponents of the doctrines of the Buddha. Sometimes they were laymen, more often monks. From the beginnings of Buddhism the 'wandering' temperament was a characteristic feature of the bikkhu, the mendicant monk. In the words of a classical formula the bikkhu 'goes from home life to the life of the homeless'. The wandering monk, driven by the resolve to break all family and social ties, turned missionary when he felt the urge to communicate to others the truth that he had received. In some cases he was influenced by the wish to broaden his experience through travel abroad. He carried his begging bowl with him (the means of his bodily sustenance) and one or more sacred books as food for his meditation and his spiritual quest. Sometimes these books were so numerous that a beast of burden was required to carry them—especially if they were accompanied by some fairly bulky statues.

3.1.3.2 These monks linked up with, or were invited to join, military or diplomatic expeditions from their homeland, or commercial caravans. Some took the Southern sea routes used by the spice trade, others the Northern land routes used by the silk trade. These expeditions had, in addition to their diplomatic or military aspects, cultural and religious significance as well. The monks who joined them were able to make their own religious contribution to the total impact made by the expedition on the foreign community to which they had journeyed.

3.1.3.3 Once they had arrived they did not remain inactive, and often enough they were the object of some curiosity. Following the example of the Master himself, Buddhist monks were tireless preachers; they chose with care the circles in which they were to preach. As they came with high diplomatic dignitaries and important international merchants, they had access to an élite of kings, princes, nobles, wealthy bourgeois and interested scholars. Very often it was the conversion of a few influential members of this élite which determined the religious choice of a whole nation.

3.1.3.4 The monks' **means of approach** were in harmony with the temperament of such an audience. They made an appeal to the fundamental anxieties, to the curiosity and to the religious yearnings often to be found amongst their listeners. This appeal followed a set pattern. First of all there was the building up of human relations, in which normally the ideal of non-violence and of friendliness, characteristic of Buddhists, played a part. To this was very often added a cultural interest, especially when the monk came from one of the two key-countries, India or China, which were considered to be culturally superior to their neighbours. The presentation of the specifically Buddhist message was undertaken by showing statues and books, followed by exposition of the basic doctrines of Buddhism—about suffering and its elimination, about the Eightfold Path, about meditation and its goal. This met with varied forms of response: agreement or questioning, or objections. Discussions were sometimes initiated and led by leading citizens of the place or even by the rulers themselves. The monastic way of life also often awakened interest.

3.1.3.5 It is important to note that usually the Buddhist message was spread by **non-violent** means. To be sure, Buddhism took advantage of the power of the great over the people, and exploited its cultural superiority, and later its economic power; but it only rarely sought to impose itself by force, and when this occurred it was the act of secular rulers. It sometimes happened that Buddhist monarchs were very strong opponents of other religions in their own territories. In Japan the most powerful monasteries, which had hundreds and even thousands of dependants, took part in the internal wars of the country. But it remains generally true that Buddhism has been and is a non-violent movement.

3.1.3.6 Nor did Buddhism insist on rigid and exclusive adherence to its doctrine by those who followed in its path. Buddhists were ready to receive local divinities into their sanctuaries and to recite sacred texts to ward off the evil spirits believed in by the common people (and others!). They accepted the support of laymen without any specific insistence upon observances other than the five basic Precepts, and the obligation to respect and to give alms to the monks. In practice Buddhism is a religion where the newcomer finds what is officially offered to him, but often also brings with him something from his previous attitudes and beliefs. Sometimes some very surprising compromises result: an Ouyghur inscription of the fourteenth century presents Genghis Khan as a beneficent 'Bodhistattva'! . . . In Kandy (Sri Lanka) there is a 'parochial' temple where a statue of Śiva, the Hindu deity, can be seen close to the central statue of the Buddha. Through all these vicissitudes, Buddhism has survived for 2,500 years and spread widely throughout southern, eastern and central Asia, giving rise to a wide variety of forms of the religious quest taking inspiration from the Buddha. We must now describe some of these forms.

## 3.2 The two 'vehicles'

Earlier, in §§1 and 2, I described the original, essential form of Buddhism which has remained substantially that of Theravada and of Southern Asia. Now I will describe three 'currents' which arose and spread out in the East and North, regions where Mahāyāna was predominant. I will call them the

(a)

(b)

*Figure 20  Different images of Buddha: (a) Golden Buddha at Wat Trimitr. (Information Service of Thailand, London);*
*(b) Reclining image of the Buddha, Natha Devale temple, Kandy (J. Allan Cash.): (c) Buddha in the lotus position. Pala (India) eleventh or twelfth century. (Crown Copyright, Victoria and Albert Museum.)*

'meditative', 'devotional' and 'militant' currents. To these we may add a fourth current, found in Tibetan and Himalayan Buddhism, which may be described as 'magical-ritual'.

### 3.2.1  The development of the meditative current in Buddhism

3.2.1.1  The origins of this aspect of Buddhism go back very far. On a seal from the third millennium BC can be found a contemplative sitting cross-legged under a tree, in the attitude now so familiar to us in representations of the Buddha. This activity was later systematized in *Yoga*; of which the very name implies 'to put together,' 'to bind' all the human faculties for the purpose of meditation; and, finally, to merge meditation with the ultimate sublime state of spiritual experience. In your study of Units 4–8 you have had some discussion of Indian Yoga, which comprises eight phases, leading on one from another to the final goal. There are two phases of moral improvement, by the elimination of vices and the acquisition of virtues. There are three phases, conditioned by the previous ones, for attaining the physical condition necessary for meditation. These phases are first, a motionless posture, statuesque yet relaxed, generally known as the 'lotus' position (*padmāsana*), like that depicted on the seal mentioned above; secondly, regulation of the breathing, which becomes slower and slower and with longer intervals; thirdly, the turning inwards of the senses, shutting out all external perception. Finally there are three truly meditative phases: first, 'binding' (*dhārana*) which involves fixing the thoughts on one single object both externally (a point, a symbol) and internally (a theme, an idea); secondly, meditation (*dhyāna*), which becomes more and more simplified, and lastly the final concentration (*samādhi*) in which all limited and determined consciousness disappears before the experience of ultimate reality.

3.2.1.2  Without neglecting the first six phases, Buddhist meditation was particularly concerned to develop the dhyāna, divided into two groups of four meditative states:

(i)  The first, 'born of solitude and of the rejection of passions, full of reflection and reasoning, leads to a state of joy and contentment'.

(ii)  The second, 'born of serenity, passes beyond reflection and reasoning, but keeps, however, joy and contentment, in an exalted tranquility'.

(iii)  In the third, 'joy and contentment are removed, remain self-controlled, in a kind of indifference (*upeksā*)', free from all disturbing consciousness.

(iv)  The fourth is the refinement and purification of the previous state until normal manifestations of human thought and sentience are totally eliminated.

3.2.1.3  Many texts insert here an exercise known as the four 'spiritual abodes' (*brahma-vihāra*), which give evidence of a more outward-looking attitude, more appropriate to the Mahāyāna ideal, than the meditative exercises just described. The contemplative passes successively through four states directed towards consideration of all beings in all parts of the world. These are: sympathetic friendliness and benevolence towards all (*maitrī*); compassion towards those who suffer (*karunā*); sharing the joy of those who are happy (*muditā*); but, ultimately (for this is only an exercise 'for getting out of oneself', and for 'forgetting one's individuality', and it must not become a disturbing desire) the contemplative must arrive at the same detachment and equanimity we have talked about in the third dhyāna (§3.2.1.2) One is therefore, according to this other procedure, brought back to the same goal of the elimination of normal consciousness.

3.2.1.4 The second series of four meditative states (*āyatana*) takes us into the field of 'non-limitation':

(v) In the fifth state, limitation is removed from the idea of space; by the blotting out of external sense-perceptions and of restricted images in the imagination, space becomes 'infinite' for the contemplative.

(vi) In the sixth, non-limitation dissolves the idea of consciousness (interior space), following the same procedure for getting rid of any specific content of mental concepts.

(vii) In the seventh, there is the fundamental negation of everything that can be regarded as *being*. This is done by repeating and experiencing the affirmation: 'Nothing exists'.

(viii) In the eighth, there is the fundamental negation not only of perception, but likewise of 'non-perception'. At this stage, the contemplative reaches the end, the ultimate cessation (nirodha; cf. Middle-Length-Sayings, I, 219). This state is indeed Nirvāna, and it defies all description and all words: 'When all constituents of being have disappeared, every object of speech, of definition, and of discussion has also disappeared' (Suttanipāta, V, 7).

Here read Horner: *Encyclopedia*, pp. 289–92, p. 331 and p. 333; and also, in the *Reader*, §§3.4.4 'The way to the highest meditations'; 3.5.2 'Emptiness'; 3.5.3 'Suchness'; and 3.5.4 'Nāgārjuna: no difference between Samsara and Nirvāna'. Now answer this question:

Which aspects of Yoga have been particularly developed in Mahāyāna Buddhism?

---

*An answer*: Especially the three phases of dhārana, dhyāna and samādhi, from which the eight states of Buddhist meditation are developed. It appears clearly from hundreds of texts, and many treatises, that meditation, its methods and its results, has been the main preoccupation of Buddhism. The whole activity in meditation tends to the annihilation of any ordinary knowledge, to reach a supreme illumination (bodhi) which cannot be described.

3.2.1.5 Notwithstanding this theoretical rejection of all analysis and definition, the Buddhists did not refrain from questioning themselves and from arguing about the nature of this 'final state' —whether it was 'empty' or 'full', negative or positive. On these points, as I have remarked, the Founder himself had been elusive, declaring that such questions or conclusions were unnecessary for the seeker who had already arrived, and dangerous for one who has not yet arrived, since he would thereby distract himself with hypothetical speculations and so relax his effort. Nevertheless disciples who wished to probe further questioned themselves and the Buddha about this Ultimate: was it a being or a state, was it positive or negative? While the Master always refused to give a clear answer, the texts of the Canon are divided into two blocks which give support to two opposite opinions on the subject (see §2.9.3.1 above).

3.2.1.6 In one series of texts it is the **negative aspect** which is stressed. All that man may try to assert with respect to the Ultimate is denied. Indeed, according to this viewpoint, the two classical terms mentioned above are both understood negatively. Nirodha means cessation, destruction, annihilation; Nirvāna is understood to mean extinction, the disappearance of a flame deprived of fuel, or blown out by the wind, as the texts explain it. Consequently some schools have strongly emphasised the negative interpretation in their technical vocabulary. This is the case with the Mādhyamika school, whose theoreticians (such as Nāgārjuna) demolish, with relentless logic, all attempts to express and even to imagine the Ultimate. It is only possible to declare it 'empty' (*Śuñya*) and to characterize its nature in terms of this same emptiness. Or again, to see clearly it is necessary to express oneself in paradoxes which demonstrate the futility of established distinctions.

> 'There is no difference at all between Samsāra and Nirvāna. There is no difference at all between Nirvāna and Samsāra'.

> 'The limit of Nirvāna is also the limit of Samsāra. Between the two, we cannot find the slightest shade of difference.'

(Nāgārjuna—see *Reader*, §3.5.4; Samsāra is the world of becoming, in which the round of transmigration or reincarnation proceeds.)

3.2.1.7 Now refer again to *Reader*, §§3.5.2 'Emptiness'; and 3.5.3 'Suchness'; also *Encyclopedia*, pp. 311–15, and *Ling*, §4.33. Then write down what you take the term 'Emptiness' or 'Void', often found in Buddhist texts, to mean.

———————◆———————

*An answer*: Buddhist meditation leads to a situation, to a state, where all normal activities cease; one arrives at a 'waning out' (Nirvāna) a cessation (*nirodha*), which these texts attempt to express only in a negative way. 'Void' is a typical word of that kind. One should note that it does not necessarily mean what *we* call 'void', or nothingness.

The philosophical school of the Mādhyamika taught that the ultimate reality of all things in the world is śūnya, empty or void, or substanceless. This Emptiness or Void (Sūnyatā) means 'an absolute transcendental reality beyond the grasp of intellectual comprehension and verbal expression' (Conze). It can be reached, however, through meditation. Since the reality of worldly phenomena and the reality of Nirvāna are the same Emptiness, it can be said that 'There is no difference between Samsāra and Nirvāna' (*Reader* §3.5.4).

3.2.1.8 Thinkers in other schools[1] bring forward objections to this negative doctrine. Is it really an absolute void, a nothingness, that is meant, or only the removal of all limits to experience? Some sages lean towards the second answer. Departing from fundamental agnosticism, there is scope for a more **positive interpretation.** To be sure, the Ultimate 'X' is of course inexpressible: there no longer exists an individual, in the usual sense of the word existence, which implies suffering. But this 'suchness' or 'thusness' (*Tathatā*) at which the Buddha has arrived (which is why he is called Tathāgata—which means 'thus arrived') is nevertheless mysteriously positive. Expressions used by the Founder which evidently support this positive

---

[1] On the rival Buddhist schools of thought, see *Ling*, §§4.33–4.35.

interpretation may be cited: Nirvāna is a 'refuge', 'another shore', an 'island', 'something immortal'. And there is that saying of the Visuddhi-Magga: 'The one who has entered Nirvāna does not exist, but Nirvāna exists'.

3.2.1.9 Reflect again on *Reader* §3.5.3 'Suchness' and then suggest why you think this word 'Suchness' (Tathatā), which occurs in several Buddhist texts, seems so obscure.

———————◆———————

*An answer*: One should not be surprised at the lack of clarity in what relates to a situation which is beyond all description. The Awakened One can only point to this situation and say: 'This', or 'So' it is,—'tatha'. The word which we translate as 'Suchness' refers to the final situation, in as much as it is experienced as positive, but which can only be realized when it is attained. Suchness is really another name for the Void. Like Void or Emptiness it suggests a state which is beyond description. It is as it is.

3.2.1.10 This determination to view Nirvāna in a positive way may be partly explicable by the innate desire to survive and even to pass beyond into 'light and happiness'. It also owes something, no doubt, to the Hindu tendency to respond to the Ultimate very positively as 'the Unique one' (*Ekam advaitiyam*), the ground of all reality, and also to the popular Hindu belief in paradise. Many disciples and several great masters and leaders of Buddhist schools had been Hindus.

3.2.1.11 In this discussion of the supreme experience the two ideas of the Void and of Fullness are put in opposition to one another, but they are also complementary. It is 'void' of all that ordinary experience might contribute to it or project into it, and from this point of view, the emptier it is, the more perfect it becomes until the ultimate is reached. On the other hand, those who think they have had the supreme experience in this life, testify that it is 'full'. This is why other names are given to it in philosophical speculation about its nature, in addition to the similes of 'refuge', 'island' etc. For example, 'Thought-Only', or 'Mind-Only' (cittamatra); 'suchness' (Tathatā); knowledge-wisdom (Prajñā).

Let us say a word more about this philosophical concept of 'Mind-Only'. This is a way of describing ultimate reality according to the Yogācāra or Vijñānavāda school. (For this read *Ling*, §4.3.5, and Conze, *Encyclopedia* p. 312.)

In describing ultimate reality as 'Mind-Only', 'Consciousness', or 'Thought-Only', the Yogācārins would seem to be among those who prefer to use more positive terms when referring to the Absolute (see §3.2.1.8 above). At the deepest level however, their ideas are not as dissimilar from those of the main 'negative' tradition as might at first appear. The Yogācārins were what we would call in Western philosophy idealists; that is, they thought that the phenomenal or external world is a product of consciousness. Consciousness, of its very nature, always perceives the world in terms of an inner subject, with which it is identified, and an outer object with which it is not: there is the 'self' and the 'not-self'. According to the Yogācārins, Nirvāna, however, consists of a state in which the dualism inherent in consciousness is transcended, and one experiences a state of pure awareness *without* an object. One can say that this state is ultimately the same as that expressed by *Emptiness* and *Suchness*.

*Figure 21  Great Bronze Buddha of Kamakura, Japan. (Popperfoto.)*

3.2.1.12 When Buddhism entered China, thinkers who sought to bring together the insights of different religions compared the positive mystery of the Buddhist 'Void-Fullness', of the 'Thought-Only', to what they already knew as the Tao, the first inexpressible principle, which has given its name to the system of Taoism. (You have an article devoted to Taoism, by Werner Eichorn in the *Encyclopedia*, pp. 374–92.) Underlying all, there is Tao, a principle unlimited in itself and thus indefinable; in the world of becoming, there is the outward manifold of fleeting, deceptive and disturbing 'realities', which it is better to abandon in order to remain in a state of outward and inward 'non-striving' (*wu wei*). This *wu wei* is, in practice, equivalent to the 'non-desire' of Buddhism. In Buddhist thought, two trends in particular developed from these roots. One, in the metaphysical realm, was basically a monistic philosophy. According to this concept, only the unique really exists; it is identified with the 'nature of the Buddha', which is immutable in itself and which cannot be expressed by us. This was the doctrine of the T'ien T'ai sect. The other trend, in the line of the spiritual quest, followed (with some adaptations and variations), the path of the dhyana, which has been briefly described above (§§3.2.1.1–3.2.1.4). This was the doctrine of the Ch'an sect. These two tendencies were to be exported from China to Korea and then to Japan. The words will be slightly modified in form: T'ien Tai will become Tendai; and Ch'an will become Zen. (On the Buddhist sects in China, read the relevant section in Robinson's article in the *Encyclopedia*, pp. 328–32, and also the Ch'an texts in the *Reader*, §3.5.5 'Chinese Sources'.)

3.2.1.13 Something must now be said about Zen. The fundamental belief in Zen Buddhism, regarding the final goal to be attained, is very positive. The mind of the ordinary man is compared to 'one who, without realizing it, is carrying a precious jewel in the folds of his garment'. Conversely, all the things that we perceive in the ordinary way are insubstantial; 'all the worlds are like a flickering flame, a shadow, a dream, a magical illusion'.[1] Likewise the attitude towards the nature of this objective is also very positively expressed; it is concerned with a beatifying enlightenment, which offers release from illusion, desire, suffering and ultimately from rebirth.

3.2.1.14 To attain this objective, Zen propounds a **method**, the rather paradoxical characteristics of which must now be indicated.

(a) As in Yoga, the suppression of the passions is first necessary in order to attain the suppression of ignorance, which is the essential point. According to the traditional wisdom of Yoga 'Ignorance is the root of all the other obstacles to enlightenment.' So too Zen affirms: 'Ignorance consists in believing in the eternity, purity, felicity and substantiality of man and of the world, whereas they are temporary, impure, unhappy, and insubstantial'; 'When ignorance disappears, freedom comes...'

(b) Both the Chinese school of Ch'an, which served as a bridge between India and Japan, and the Japanese school of Zen (under its two forms Rinzai and Sōtō) affirm with one voice that the secret of enlightenment cannot be conveyed by prayer or ritual. In this they remain faithful to the inspiration of the Buddha, who declared that the existence or non-existence of the gods was irrelevant for followers of his method.

(c) The same applies with regard to books and texts. In so far as they are made up of words, incapable of expressing true reality, and are confined within limited systems which cannot enclose actual experience, written texts cannot 'pass through the door'. At best they help one to stand expectantly on the threshold to await the opening of the door.

(d) Guidance from a master who has already had the essential experience is, on the other hand indispensable. But even a master feels the entanglement of words. Consequently his aim will be to by-pass them and to show the way, beyond words, to lived experience. He will receive the disciple, he will set him on the path towards the goal of the quest and, above all, he will wrench him away from reliance upon intellectual methods. He will respond to 'intelligent' questions either by silence, or by apparently absurd expressions; he will sometimes respond to respect with coarseness or brutality, to the wish for contact by an apparently bored muteness. At other times he will, on the contrary, be a model of kindness. His conduct will be 'irrational' in order to suggest the 'supra-rational'.

(e) One of the ways to overthrow reason will be to put to it, as a topic of thought, a form of expression which is in itself apparently absurd. Enigmatic questions of this kind are termed *kōan*. For example: 'You know the noise made by two hands clapping. What is the noise made by one hand?'... 'You ask what is the Buddha? Three pounds of flax!.... 'What do you do if you meet the Buddha? Kill him'... We find some paradoxes of this kind in

---

[1] Suzuki, B. L. (1969) *Mahāyāna Buddhism*, Allen & Unwin, London, p. 113.

Nāgārjuna (*Reader*, §3.5.4); we have Chinese kōans (*Reader*, §3.5.5, 'Chinese sources'), and Japanese kōans[1] (see *Encyclopedia*, p. 333, and *Ling*, §5.23). English words to translate kōan might be: enigma, riddle or paradox— something which baffles the ordinary logical or common-sense workings of the mind. Kōan originated in the paradoxical sayings of the early Zen masters. Eventually these were collected and, particularly in the Rinzai sect in Japan, have been systematized into a progressive sequence to aid the seeker to enlightenment.

(f) In order to dwell on reflections of this kind, or rather to eliminate all reflections, lengthy sessions of meditation (zazen) are undertaken in carefully arranged conditions. There is withdrawal into oneself, silence, immobility, natural light, correction by a supervisor if one relaxes; these meditation exercises may continue for seven or eight hours a day.

(g) In this way a state of tense expectation is created which, through the extinction of reasoning, perception and movement, may lead to a sudden enlightenment. One cannot foresee the manner of this enlightenment, whether it will take a short or a long time, whether it will be extraordinary or prosaic. As sudden as the clang of a bell breaking the silence, or the leap of a frog in a pond, the moment of *satori*, enlightenment, breaks through.

(h) According to Zen, whoever achieves satori will thenceforward possess a special light which colours his life and shows its previously hidden depths: 'To walk becomes Zen, to work becomes Zen, to rest becomes Zen'.

Zen schools were not very numerous or active until fairly recent times; today, however, especially in Japan, a significantly large number of Buddhists are following this way (here look at *Reader*, §3.5.6 'Japanese Sources'). As an appendix to these units you will find a further treatment of Japanese Zen, written by Margaret Hall (§6).

## 3.2.2  The development of the devotional current

3.2.2.1 From the early days of Buddhism, however, it was apparent that this 'way' of enlightenment, austere and daunting, could not appeal to everyone. Very soon another trend emerged, which reached its fullest development in the 'devotion' towards the Buddha fostered by the Japanese movements known as Jōdō and Shinshu, drawing on the religious heritage of India and China (*Encyclopedia*, pp. 339–40; Ling, §6.48).

The initial inspiration came from India. The Buddha had forbidden the monks to concern themselves with his ashes and his funeral and warned them not to propagate a 'cult' in his respect: 'After me your master will be the doctrine itself (Dhamma); you will be your own lamp'. Nevertheless, with his usual clear-sightedness, and already realizing the respect with which he had been surrounded during his life, the Buddha foresaw that his disciples would make much of his funeral rites; he tolerated the prospect that his lay followers would do so. In fact it was not only laymen, but pious monks—eminent as well as lowly monks—who gradually introduced a 'transfiguration' of the Founder and an attitude of prayerful respect towards him. According to an old maxim, 'It is hard to have no one to worship and to invoke' (see the texts on 'Personal Devotion', *Reader*, §§3.6.1, the introductory texts and 3.6.2 'Infallibility of the Buddha').

---

[1] Suzuki, D. T. (1955) *Manual of Zen Buddhism*, Hutchinson, London.

3.2.2.2 The beginning of this change is already discernible in a Sanskrit text (which was to become most important for this line of development), entitled the *Saddharmapundarikasutra*, or 'The Lotus of the True Law' (*Reader* §3.6.3). In this text a Buddha appears who has in some way survived his disappearance from the earth, and manifests in himself two of the characteristics most frequently used in religious imagery to indicate happiness and immortality. He is 'Boundless *Life*' (*Amitāyus*) and 'Boundless *Light*' (*Amitābha*). The Sanskrit term *Amita* (in Chinese, *O-mi-to*, and in Japanese, *Amida*), became by itself a proper noun given to one particular Buddha in one particular context. (Now look at *Reader*, §3.6.4 'Meaning and power of the Sacred Names'.)

3.2.2.3 I have used the expression 'one particular Buddha'. This no doubt raises some questions in your minds, which are worth reflecting upon here. Is there more than one Buddha, and if so what is the relationship between other Buddhas and *the* Buddha? What could account for development of belief in a multiplicity of Buddhas? And what is to be understood by the term, which occurs in this connection, '*Bodhisattva*'?

Following the inclinations of Indian religious devotion, Buddhist belief came to accept that there had been a large number of glorious and propitious Buddhas. There are many Buddhas, for each world and for each era. There have been many Buddhas in this world, both preceding and following Gautama. It is believed that in the future another Buddha must come, whose very name implies his function: Maitreya, 'The Compassionate One'. All those Buddhas who have already come and gone appear to maintain an active interest in, and sympathy for, the spiritual efforts of men still in this life.

3.2.2.4 According to some schools, all the Buddhas are only different manifestations of a 'fundamental' Buddha; perhaps there is, underlying all, simply the nature of Buddha itself, without a personal reality. To some, moreover, it seems a contradictory idea to suppose that the Buddhas must 'come down again' from their mysterious and fundamentally different state, to make active interventions in favour of men, and to come into contact with beings immersed in the limited world of matter. So a doctrine was developed which puts this intervention 'outside' the ultimate state. There are two ways in which this doctrine is presented.

3.2.2.5 First, it is explained that the Buddhas, after their enlightenment on earth, decide to remain among men for some time (just as *the* Buddha of our world period did), as long as they judge to be necessary. They are able to do so since their destiny is now at their own disposal. They use this time to help their contemporaries by their presence, example and preaching, until the time when at last they choose to die physically and to attain the supreme 'surcease' (*parinirvāna*).

3.2.2.6 Secondly a belief emerges, more and more clearly, in the existence of personages who act as intermediaries between, on the one hand those beneficent Buddhas who have attained to parinirvāna and the final state, and, on the other hand, suffering humanity. These personages, already enlightened but still in contact with men and at their service in this way, are called Bodhisattva (in Pali, *Bodhisatta*; in Japanese, *Bosatsu*). They are very active in this world, even though to act here they must come down from some paradise to our level. Some of them are much invoked by devotees. This is particularly the case with one of the two bodhisattvas who serve in this way as acolytes to the Buddha Amida. This bodhisattva originated in India, and is mentioned elsewhere in the text of the Saddharmapundarikasūtra already referred to in §3.2.2.2 above. He bears the significant name of Avalokitesvara, 'The Lord who lowers his gaze'—that is, who looks down on men with compassion and with the will to help them. He passed into China under the name of Kwan-Yin, and came to Japan as Kwannon. The feminine sex is sometimes ascribed to this bounteous and enigmatic figure, who is shown with appropriate accompaniments, such as a child in her arms or a flower in her hand. The Buddha Amida and the Bodhisattva Kwannon have been the object of great veneration and trustful prayer from India to Japan.

3.2.2.7 Following the model of the enlightened ones who remain for a while longer on earth, or those who come back to earth to preach liberation and to help mortals to its attainment, the most altruistic monks embraced the ideal of devoting themselves to the liberation of others. They proclaim:

> An immense compassion and a heart full of pity, this is what being Buddha truly means. Compassion is the Buddha, and the Buddha is compassion'.

(B. L. Suzuki (1969) *op cit*, p. 117)

*Figure 22  Bodhisattva Padmapani. Painting from Cave 1 Ajanta, India c.600–700 CE. (Mansell Collection)*

They make the Bodhisattva's Vow, and for the sake of those who are bereft of refuge and salvation, they take humanity under their care, and become themselves its refuge and salvation.

For further study of this subject, refer to the following texts in the *Reader*: §3.6.5, 'Devotion to Amida'; 3.6.6 'The commitment of the Bodhisattva for the salvation of men'; 3.6.7 'Explanation and praise of the Bodhisattva Avalokitesvara'; and 3.6.8 'How should one preach the Saddharmapundarika-sutra?'. Read also *Ling*, pp. 140–1, and especially the relevant section in the article by E. Conze (*Encyclopedia*, pp. 297–308) on 'The Bodhisattva ideal' and 'Mythological doctrines'.

3.2.2.8 This devotional current has given birth to two Japanese schools (Jōdō, Shinshu) which have proved very attractive. Their founders and leaders were 'charismatic' figures of great influence (for example, the Japanese reforming saint Hōnen, 1133–1212 CE; see *Encyclopedia*, pp. 339–40). Their religious conceptions were more theistic and devotional than those of Zen. The faithful strive to imitate these great masters and to obtain the same spiritual favours that were bestowed upon them.

(a) The decisive spiritual attitude, according to these schools, is that of trustful faith. 'Believe therefore, open yourselves to receive; doubt neither me nor the blessed Buddhas', so it is written in the Vyuhā.

(b) If one hopes to be reborn in a heavenly destiny, it is not as a reward for good works, but on account of the help of the Buddhas and of faith: 'Even

*Figure 23   Kwan-Yin (Avalokitesvara) China Sung period. (Museum van Aziatische Kunst, Amsterdam.)*

one who, for his wicked deeds, deserves to fall into hell, will, if he hearkens to Amitāyus and practises faith in him, be reborn in bliss' (Vyuhā).

(c) This faith is expressed and practised through a special observance (which has parallels in many other religions)—namely, the repeated invocation of the name of the particular Buddha who is being honoured. In this case the practice comes from India, where it was directed to the Hindu gods—the *japa*. It was transferred to Buddhism and eventually to Japan. Recitation of the formula '*Namo Amida Buddha*', 'reverence to the Buddha Amida', carries with it some extraordinary promises of future liberation: 'If any son or daughter will hear the name and, with all thought stilled, will keep it in mind for one, two, three, four, five, six, or seven nights...when they come to die, the Tathagata will stand before them...and they will be reborn in the Happy Land (Sukhāvatī)'. It is likewise by the invocation of the name that the sinner who relies on trustful faith in Amida will also be able to be reborn into happiness—in the 'Pure Land', the 'Paradise of the West', the domain where Amida receives his own, and whence one eventually passes to the final Nirvāna.

(d) The most devoted followers may expect to be favoured with visions of Amida. Hōnen, one of the greatest masters of this religious school, affirmed in all sincerity that this had been vouchsafed to himself. This saintly Japanese monk, after many complicated and unfruitful spiritual experiments, undertaken especially from the standpoint of Tendai monism (see *Encyclopedia*, pp. 338–9), had discovered, practised and propagated the 'simple way' of faith in and invocation of the name of Amida. He said: 'The present times are too far away from the Master and so this is a period of decadence. No one is any longer able to attain the depths of wisdom. All that people are still capable of is an act of faith in the Buddha!' He also used to say of Amida: 'His light penetrates the world in all directions. His grace is never denied to those who call upon him.'

(e) The affirmations of Hōnen, and still more those of certain disciples who simplified this message, have provoked strong reactions. This was to be expected, since Buddhism was originally a method of auto-salvation. The last message of the Buddha was: 'Work out your own salvation with diligence' and the doctrinal tendency represented by the Amida cult seemed instead to offer reward to those who relied on passivity and trusted that salvation would be bestowed upon them. The Amida Buddhists respond to such an objection with two main considerations: in the first place they point out that their claims must not be exaggerated, and that their true doctrine is not to be confused with the more extravagant beliefs of some followers; they also explain that, in real life, faith and works are in fact inseparable if a man is sincere and logical. A man 'without works' and determined to remain as such will not reach the depth of true faith: the will to make 'spiritual' progress and the ability to involve oneself in 'works' is an indivisible quality in life. Conversely, a man 'without faith' will not be able to maintain his good works. Again, true faith can only be born, live and grow in association with good works, and vice versa. It should be noted that for some Amida Buddhists, as an exception to the more usual assumption in Buddhism marriage is not considered as an obstacle and a hindrance to attaining Nirvāna. For instance, one of Hōnen's favourite disciples, Shinran (1173–1262) the founder of Shinshu, sought to follow his religious vocation in the married state, considering that celibacy could lead to spritual pride (see *Encyclopedia*, p. 340).

### 3.2.2.9 Question

Now refer to the following texts in *Reader*, §3.6.2 'Infallibility of the Buddha'; 3.6.3 'The authority of the Saddharmapundarikasūtra'; and 3.6.5 'Devotion to Amida'. Then try your hand at answering this question: What do these texts reveal about the different meanings of 'faith' in the Buddhism of the Theravada and the Buddhism of the devotees of Amida and of the Pure Land sects?

PLEASE PAUSE HERE

DO NOT READ ON UNTIL YOU HAVE COMPLETED THE EXERCISE

### 3.2.2.10 Specimen answer and discussion

The Buddhist word *saddhā*, translated as 'faith', does not mean what 'faith' often means in Western religious language. The Buddhist saddhā does not demand beliefs in certain truths simply because a god or master has proposed them; the Buddha himself said that his disciples should submit his message to the test of each one's experience, which would pass the final judgement. However, till one has arrived at that personal verification, the Master and his word deserve respect, and should be accepted as entirely trustworthy. It is in this restricted sense that 'faith' is understood in the Theravada tradition.

Clearly, however, the 'faith' practised by the devotees of Amida and in the Pure Land sects is of a quite different kind. It is not the kind of 'faith' one has in a good revered teacher who can but 'point the way', but a faith in the saving powers of a supernatural being, such as one finds in theistic religions. In the case of the 'Lotus of the True Law' the sutra itself takes on this saving power. In Japanese two words are used to denote the two different ways of attaining salvation. In the Zen sect the way is that of *jiriki*—'self-power'. In the Jōdō and Shin sects, the way is through *tariki*—'other power'.

To sum up then, one may say that Amida Buddhism, without making Amida a personal and transcendent God as in more clearly monotheistic religions (e.g. Judaism, Christianity, Islam) is nevertheless the Japanese mode of religious thought which most nearly approximates to monotheism, particularly among the simple and unsophisticated believers. One must remember, however, that followers of this form of Buddhism believe that, beyond Amida and Paradise, the ultimate goal remains, of course, Nirvāna.

### 3.2.3 The 'militant' current

There have been other Japanese sects which have been influential to a great or lesser extent. I will make special mention here of one of them in particular because its militant character may seem to be at variance with the Buddhist idea of non-violence. It is the sect which bears the name of its founder, Nichiren (1222–82 CE, see *Encyclopedia*, p. 340).

3.2.3.1 Nichiren was the son of a poor fisherman. In his youth he was worried by the problem of personal salvation, and the fact that prayers could go unanswered in spite of their fervour. His character attracted others to him, but was marked with a rather fanatical zeal, which made him a judge of his contemporaries, a reformer and a prophet. He was persecuted and twice exiled. He set himself up as a purifier of Buddhism, teaching a doctrine based on monistic principles, according to which one must strive to realize in oneself the 'nature of the Buddha present and hidden in all'. His reforming programme aimed at achieving not only personal progress and happiness, but also the good order and prosperity of society and of the State. Social and national fulfilment could proceed only from the doctrinal purity and moral orthodoxy which he proclaimed.

3.2.3.2 Since preaching did not seem to be sufficient to bring about the desired reform the members of the sect chose to become militant and even intolerant. Consequently one finds them in the fifteenth century as 'soldier-monks' in revolt; in the sixteenth century they organised what amounted to a veritable crusade, but it proved abortive. During the revival of Japanese nationalism in the nineteenth century, the sect maintained close contact with the military, who were its central core. At the present time a highly committed offshoot of Nichiren, called Sōka-Gakkai, has entered the political arena and formed its own party, the Kōmeitō (see below, §4.4.2.9). It attacks corruption in political life, and has scored great success.

3.2.3.3 At first sight this militant character of the sect seems astonishing, when one recalls that the first Buddhist commandment enjoins non-violence One may look for explanations on a theoretical level, by saying, for example, that the defence and the propagation of the true doctrine allows, indeed demands, the extirpation of errors, but this is not very convincing. Really, it is simpler to think that the monasteries had become political powers and had given way to the temptation to play a worldly role by worldly means; that the monks, too easily recruited and leading too easy a life, came to work for the progress of Buddhism using political criteria and adopting political perspectives.

### 3.2.4 The distinctive character of Tibetan Buddhism

Tibetan Buddhism does not draw from one current alone; as we shall see, it does not even draw its beliefs and practices from traditional Buddhism alone; one finds in it elements from pre-Buddhist beliefs and practices as well as from the currents within Buddhism which we have been studying. There has also been, in the course of centuries, an infiltration of elements from Hindu sources.

3.2.4.1 Before the arrival of Buddhism, there existed in Tibet an indigenous cult commonly called the 'Bon' religion. This embraced a multitude of elements inherited from ancient times when the inhabitants had been polyandrous, and their religion contained many magical and superstitious observances. The ancient Tibetans believed in vital, mysterious forces residing in human flesh, blood and bodily juices, which could be absorbed and put to use by others, and which could be obtained even from a corpse or from spilt blood, provided that they were still fresh. There were legends of primordial heroes, ancestors of the race, from whom the rulers were supposed to be descended. When the rulers died there were ceremonies which enabled their souls to rejoin their ancestors.

Gods were held to live especially at the summit of the great Himalayan mountains, which were therefore sacred. There were also many demons. Powers for good or evil were possessed by magicians who knew secret spells and at times put themselves into ecstatic trances.

### 3.2.4.2 Exercise

Such was the religious situation encountered by Buddhism when it first arrived in Tibet in the seventh century CE (see *Ling*, §5.27). Tibetan

Buddhism took the form, principally, of Tantrism—which had originated in India. I will ask you to find out what this word refers to. What are 'Tantras', and what are they used for? For material for your answer, read *Ling*, §5.26; *Encyclopedia*, p. 296; and the following passages in the *Reader*, §§3.7.1 'Some introductory notes on ritual and magic in Tibet'; 3.7.2 'Tibetan invocations'; 3.7.3 'The cult of the Goddess Tara'; and 3.7.4 'An Evocation of Prajñaparamita'.


### PLEASE PAUSE HERE
DO NOT READ ON UNTIL YOU HAVE COMPLETED THE EXERCISE


### 3.2.4.3 Specimen answer and discussion

'Tantras' are texts said to have been revealed by the Buddha from the heights of his transcendent existence, or by other Buddhas who entrusted the secret wisdom to the first of a line of gurus. Their importance and their force lies in their magical efficacy. 'They contain magical spells, descriptions of divinities and sets of incantations arranged for meditational and ritual use, instructions in sacramental worship and in the bestowing of consecretations'.[1] The expected effect of the Tantric rituals is the acquisition of earthly blessings, a good rebirth and even the attainment of Nirvāna in this life; they are also the means to acquire extraordinary powers. These powers enable their possessor to exercise telepathy, thought-reading and levitation, and other marvellous feats—thus exciting great admiration among the people. Each Tantric system is taught by a master to chosen disciples.

---

3.2.4.4 In this esoteric discipline the master holds the central place,[2] as he does of course in non-Tantric Buddhism too.

> 'Will one gain release, abiding in meditation?
>
> What is the use of lamps? What is the use of offerings
>
> What's to be done by reliance on mantras? ...
> (But) If the word of one's master but enter the heart,
> It is like a treasure in the palm of one's hand.'

3.2.4.5 The subsequent history of Tibetan Buddhism has been marked by great changes, by persecution and by some reforming movements. A considerable number of sects developed. There was a great increase in the number of monks whose life was at times somewhat irregular by traditional standards; some were not duly ordained, some were married.

3.2.4.6 Religious activity in Tibet remained Buddhist in the sense that it was exercised by Buddhist monks; but the various kinds of activity were sometimes outside the paths of traditional Buddhism. For instance, monks celebrated innumerable ceremonies to ward off evil spirits, to avert disasters, to obtain fecundity for women, to ensure a happy passage to the deceased, and to secure for both living and dead a happy rebirth. Faithful layfolk and monks repeat endlessly the mysterious formula: *Om mani padme hum*, 'the jewel

---

[1] Snellgrove, D. (1957) *Buddhist Himalaya*, Cassirer, Oxford, p. 55.

[2] Quoted in Conze, E. *et al* (1954) *Buddhist texts through the Ages*, Cassirer, Oxford.

*Figure 24(a) Old Tibetan twirls his prayer wheel, Darjeeling, India. (Douglas Dickins.)*

*Figure 24(b) Tibetan woman with rosary. In the background are the prayer wheels of Vica Chhwelling Monastery, Ghoom near Darjeeling. (Douglas Dickins.)*

Figure 24(c)   Tibetan wheel of life, Bhavachakra, nineteenth century. (Crown Copyright, Victoria and Albert Museum.)

Figure 24(d)   Meditation centre, Boulder, Colorado following Tibetan Buddhist ideas. (Christopher Schwarz.)

in the lotus' (cf. *Reader*, §3.7.1), which can have a purely spiritual meaning of putting oneself back into the wisdom of the Buddha, or—in some groups—a sexual meaning sublimated into the spiritual experience. The use of efficacious incantations (mantra) became more popular, likewise the contemplation of sacred designs (mandala) with a symbolic meaning which cannot be understood without possessing the key to their meaning (cf. *Ling*, §5.26).

The public rituals of Tibet have become well known through the descriptions and photographs of Western observers; the long bellowing horns, the ritual dances, the use of prayer-mills, the lengthy services of homage and recital. There are also 'trance' seances, a strange phenomenon in which clairvoyant powers and hypnosis are combined with experiments in respiratory control and spiritual concentration. Another preoccupation in Tibetan Buddhism is the recounting and interpretation of dreams.

3.2.4.7 Buddhist Tibet eventually evolved into a monastery-state where the monks, under the Dalai Lama and the Panchen Lama, were, from their monastery-fortresses, at one and the same time temporal and spiritual masters (see *Ling*, §6.49). All that was brought to an end with the occupation of Tibet by Communist China. Is it the end of this long chapter in Buddhist history?

### 3.2.4.8 Exercise

As an exercise to revise this survey of Buddhism in Tibet, write down what you take to be the chief respects in which Tibetan Buddhism differs from the older and more traditional forms of Buddhism elsewhere. In addition to revising what you have read already, now read what Conze says about the special characteristics of Tantric Buddhism (*Encyclopedia*, pp. 314–5).

PLEASE PAUSE HERE

DO NOT READ ON UNTIL YOU HAVE COMPLETED THE EXERCISE

### 3.2.4.9 Specimen answer

Tibetan Buddhism shows many contrasts to early and traditional Buddhism elsewhere. Even if the objectives are substantially the same—a passage to happy rebirths, followed by passing to Nirvāna—attitudes and methods have become profoundly different. The cult of a multiplicity of superhuman beings (often feared), amongst whom the feminine element has found a place, has replaced indifference towards the world of the devas. The path of meditation has been obscured by a host of magical or hypnotic practices. The extraordinary and sensational powers of the enlightened, which the Buddha had not denied (although he had always discouraged the public and vainglorious display of them) are here the object of curiosity and intense esteem, something to be sought after. Through Tantrism the original monastic celibacy, the rejection of sexual activity and of situations which could lead to it, give place at times to the use of sexual activity as a means of attaining the final fulfilment. Union with a woman becomes both a symbol and a means of reaching union with ultimate wisdom.

### 3.2.5 Conclusion

We have considered four main currents in the wider development of Buddhism: meditative, devotional, militant and magical-ritual. Buddhist belief and practice have distinctive characteristics, which I have endeavoured to bring out in the first part of these units. But it is not possible to conceive of Buddhism as a firmly-structured system. Different interpreters have modified the traditional doctrines and customs with great freedom. The vicissitudes of history have brought other changes. It is more suitable to regard Buddhism as an entire 'world' to itself rather than as a single clearly-defined system. Popular devotion plays an important part in shaping this 'world', as we shall have occasion to remark in the final part of these units.

# 4 TRANSFORMATIONS: BUDDHISM AND THE PRESENT-DAY SITUATION

## 4.1 Introduction

We have seen that as Buddhism extended the geographical area of its influence and developed its ideas it became diversified according to the social, cultural and political systems with which it came into contact. It was able to enter into new environments by adapting itself. This has led to the creation of relationships and exchanges between Buddhism and the systems it has encountered at all levels—economic, intellectual, artistic, political and religious.

In all these various transformations one factor seems often to have been of cardinal importance: a close alliance between Buddhist 'religious' society (the Sangha) and 'secular' socio-political society (the State). The success of Buddhism amongst the people in general has, to a large extent, stemmed from this alliance. Buddhism desires that the whole State be governed basically in accord with the precepts of the Dhamma. The State would thus, first and foremost, become a vehicle of spiritual progress towards deliverance.

For their part the monarchs who adopted Buddhism wished to derive from it, and often did, not only personal spiritual progress but the consecration of their kingship. Buddhism was a moral support aiding them in the education of the people. This system of alliance (which amounted, on occasion, almost to the union of the secular and religious 'state') was both a source of great strength, but also of danger to the religious ideas of Buddhism. It is of course true that as a consequence Buddhism had the support of the temporal powers and that this meant that material needs were met and that Buddhist monks were free to concentrate on their spiritual quest. Moreover, the prestige and the privileged position which Buddhism enjoyed greatly encouraged its expansion amongst the people at large. On the other hand, however, this union involved a large number of monks and entire monasteries in political matters and risked distracting them from their life of contemplation and detachment from the world. What is more, the success of Buddhism was thenceforth conditional upon the success of its protectors—their decline might well precipitate its decline also.

Modern sociologists have strongly emphasised this aspect of Buddhist society, but it does not in itself explain everything; like any other movement Buddhism has flourished or declined first and foremost because of the spiritual enthusiasm or decadence of its members and particularly its monks. But it is of course evident that right up until modern times the impact upon Buddhism of secular conditions (economic, intellectual, political) has been great. This relationship between religious and secular society in the Buddhist world, and its effects, is a connecting thread running through the account which follows. Since we cannot here examine the features of Buddhism in all countries today, we will limit ourselves to a consideration of three environments in each of which its position is distinctively different. In the first, *Sri Lanka*, Buddhism enjoys, at the present time, a position of privilege. In the second, *China*, it is persecuted. In the third, *Japan*, the State keeps itself at a distance, but recognizes the fact of Buddhism's existence. The consequences of these three attitudes are both various and interesting.

## 4.2 Sri Lanka: Buddhism in a privileged position

### 4.2.1 Historical background

4.2.1.1 In your set book, Trevor Ling summarizes what is known about the origins and early history of Buddhism in Sri Lanka or Ceylon (*Ling*, §§3.27, 4.38, 4.39 and 5.29). In another book[1] the same author remarks that from the time of the first Buddhist mission to Ceylon a triple alliance was formed between the monastic Sangha, the king who made himself its lay protector and the people who followed their sovereign's choice, whilst retaining, nevertheless, many former beliefs.

4.2.1.2 One general psychological factor favouring the success of Buddhism in Ceylon was the respect of the Sinhalese for Indian culture, and their consideration for the glory and power of the Emperor Aśoka. This certainly paved the way for his son, the first Buddhist missionary to the island. Moreover, the first Buddhists did not condemn existing beliefs but simply affirmed that the new way they were presenting was better and definitive. They maintained a living bond with Indian Buddhism (even to the extent of transplanting a part of the sacred Bodhi tree). They responded to the needs and preferences of the masses by building great religious structures and by organizing ceremonies. They did not neglect the place of women, who were provided with instruction from a nun, herself a daughter of Aśoka.

4.2.1.3 In his book, *Religion and Ideology in Sri Lanka*[2] F. Houtart has noted that colonization—particularly by the British—whilst respecting the status quo, nevertheless (by reducing the power of the Buddhist kings to almost nothing) also enormously weakened the position of Buddhism itself. Buddhism might even have disappeared, but it survived precisely to the extent to which the Sangha, the monastic order, organized in major groupings (*nikāyas*), retained a cohesion of its own, and a certain economic, social and cultural 'autonomy' (see *Ling*, §7.40).

4.2.1.4 Thus by remaining as witnesses to the authentic past of the country the Sangha became, successively, 'the base of an attempted political re-establishment, the booster and instrument at the service of nationalism, a privileged religion in the independent Republic.'[3] In the struggle for independence, Buddhist monks and monasteries had the function of symbolizing the national aspirations and served in a way as the 'national conscience'.

4.2.1.5 They have now been rewarded by the recovery of a certain number of privileges, notably a greatly increased participation in the educational system. This is to be seen in the presence almost everywhere of Buddhist institutions and teachers. The pro-Buddhist state has undertaken an overhaul of the school system which had hitherto been 'westernized' and marked by the influence of Christianity; the new system is an expression of the influence of the Buddhist majority.

4.2.1.6 Rather surprisingly, however (or so it would seem at first sight), despite their privileged position, the monks are not necessarily always in agreement with the State. Houtart rightly draws attention to reasons for deep-felt opposition which may arise in certain situations. Confronted with a

---

[1] Ling, T. (1973) *The Buddha*, Temple Smith, London.

[2] Houtart, F. (1974) *Religion and Ideology in Sri Lanka*, Hansa Publications, Colombo, p. 467.

[3] Houtart, F. (1974) *ibid.*

*Figure 25 Temple of the Tooth, Dalada Maligawa, Kandy, Ceylon. (J. Allan Cash.)*

State which insists on its paramount power and which, like many modern states, tends to diminish the freedom of thought, expression and action of the individual, and his independence of conscience and personal initiative, Buddhism has retained its basic concern for the individual in its deepest spiritual aims. 'Be for yourself your own light'. Thus in recent protests 'the (Buddhist) factor has gained new weight in the political field, through its function of individual protest'.[1]

Let us move now from general sociological considerations to an examination of Buddhism in Ceylon, especially in its popular forms.

### 4.2.2 Buddhism in Sri Lanka today

4.2.2.1 On present estimates more than 60 per cent of Ceylonese are Buddhists, 20 per cent Hindus, more than 8 per cent Christian and more than 6 per cent Moslem. There has been a tendency since independence for

[1] Houtart, F. (1974) *ibid.*, p. 492.

some of those who had previously been uncertain to commit themselves more fully to Buddhism. A Ceylonese scholar, A. Fernando, who is professor of Buddhism at one of his country's universities, considers that one must distinguish between two kinds of Buddhism in Sri Lanka. There is a popular form which is 'simply a Sinhalese version of Shamanism and in which the village leaders (the *kattandiya*) preside over ritual cults addressed to gods and demons'. There is also an official orthodox Buddhism 'having as its central core Buddhist monasticism.'[1]

4.2.2.2 Fernando describes 'Shamanism' as a religion which is based on a belief in the existence of secondary deities and the power of the cult-leaders (the Shamans) to appease them. In Ceylon this popular religion has its doctrine, its cult objects, its priests, its prayers, its chants. But it is not recognized officially—indeed, in theory, the worship of gods and goddesses is considered as useless, and to be discouraged. Nevertheless, there is scarcely a temple which does not dedicate a chapel, or at the very least an altar or a statue to some deity or other. Popular belief is that these deities, either benevolent or malevolent, have a direct influence on ordinary life; it is by certain prescribed rituals that their favour can be obtained or their hostility counteracted. In this popular pantheon the deified Buddha reigns together with Sakka (the great god Indra of Hindu origin); they are surrounded by Vishṇu, Skandha, etc., and a series of hostile powers (including spirits of the dead) who can bring misfortune, despite the watchful protection of the Four Guardians of the points of the compass. This pantheon has been described at length by L. A. de Silva,[2] who also makes it clear that despite the important position of these devas they remain on a lower level and subordinate to the Buddha.

Most of all, the people fear *demons*, which are often identified with the spirits of departed personages of importance, for example, kings and princes. When an illness does not respond to medical treatment this is often attributed to the interference of a demon, the result of an evil spell cast by a malevolent neighbour. In order to overcome the effects of such a spell, the monks perform a variety of ceremonies, according to the nature of the illness, which can last as long as seven days.

4.2.2.3 This intermingling of Buddhist and other religious cultures is an extremely old phenomenon and there is every indication that it will persist. De Silva has shown that in pre-Buddhist Ceylon the Yāksha (spirits dwelling in trees, mountains and rivers) were already honoured. Even trees themselves were worshipped, which explains why the transplanted branch of the Tree of Enlightenment (Bodhi tree), brought by the first missionaries, easily won a place in the spiritual esteem and the worship of the Ceylonese.[3] Homage was rendered to ancestors and to the great departed, just as it was later to be rendered to the Buddha and his images[4]. Memorial tumuli (*stūpa, thūpa*) were heaped up over the relics of such great personages, just as they were to be raised over the relics of the Buddha.[5]

4.2.2.4 Festivals are another aspect of popular religion. These are numerous, and they manifest the same intermingling of the old and the new. There are

[1] Fernando, A. (1970) in Dumoulin, H. (ed) 'Buddhism im heutigen Ceylon', in *Buddhismus der Gegenwuart*, p. 38.
[2] De Silva, L. A. (1974) *Buddhism, Beliefs and Practices in Sri Lanka*, Christian Study Centre Division of Buddhist Studies, Colombo, pp. 127–142.
[3] De Silva, L. A. (1974) *ibid.*, pp. 45–47.
[4] De Silva, L. A. (1974) *ibid.*, pp. 47–57.
[5] De Silva, L. A. (1974) *ibid.*, pp. 42–44.

(a)

(b)

(c)

*Figure 26  Pilgrimage to Adam's Peak, Ceylon:*
*(a) Gateway at the foot of Adam's Peak;*
*(b) Adam's Peak with pilgrims ascending and*
*descending after spending a night on the peak;*
*(c) and (d) Offerings at the spot on the summit bearing*
*the impression of the Buddha's foot; (e) The mountain*
*at sunrise as the pilgrim sees it; (f) The descent.*
*(Bury Peerless.)*

(d)

(e)

(f)

festivals known as the *Ásala Perahara*, which honour in one and the same way the minor deities of old and the relic of the Tooth of the Buddha at Kandy. The Vesak Festival commemorates simultaneously the birth, enlightenment and death of the Buddha since these are all held to have occurred in the same month of the year. The Posan Festival commemorates the introduction of Buddhism into Ceylon. Old and new customs are combined in the New Year Festival[1]. Pilgrimages (which are a cherished feature of all the religions of the island) are made not only to the great and unique Buddhist sites of India, but also to holy places in Ceylon itself. One of these, Adam's Peak, is a place of pilgrimage for Hindus, Buddhists, Christians and Moslems alike. It is a massive symbol of the religious pluralism of Ceylon.

4.2.2.5

> Orthodox Buddhism has never given official approval to this popular form of the religion, but it has allowed it to grow upon itself like a kind of parasitic vegetation . . . The two have developed for so long together that in the eyes of the simple masses they form a single organism. It is by no means impossible, as often happens, that the parasite has absorbed some of the sap and the life-force of the tree that supports it.
>
> (Fernando, A. (1970) *op. cit.* p. 61.)

### 4.2.2.6 Exercise

In the following passages[2] three explanations are given of the motives underlying an apparently non-Buddhist phenomenon—prayer. When you have read them summarize briefly what, according to the author, are those three motives which move many Buddhists to pray.

> Of course many of the laymen make petitions of their own to the Buddha. This, however, is not logically consistent with the orthodox theory of the Buddha's present condition—for he is in Nirvāna beyond all touch of change and Samsāra. Many of the laymen know this, yet in religious and non-theoretical moments pray to him just the same. If they are careful to retain their consistency, yet wish to make petitional prayers, they will place their requests (as even the monks do) not before the Buddha but before the nats or the devatas. This, however, a monk in Galle told me, has nothing to do with religion. It is a matter of business—one contracts with the devata for this assistance, agreeing that when the requested aid is actually given, one will make an offering to the Buddha and transfer the merit thus acquired to the devata. It is, said he, no more religion than is dealing with the government. Religion has to do with the Teacher.
>
> Some Buddhists pray, that is repeat sacred verses, because, as they believe, the Buddha has commanded that his followers should do so; and if they do so with a pure heart they will receive a blessing in return. In strict theory, however, the intelligent Buddhist prays because of the good subjective effects which the act of prayer produces in his own mind and character . . .
>
> A monk in Rangoon said to me, 'Prayer and offering are not received by the Buddha in the sense that they have any effect upon him, nor in

---

[1] De Silva, L. A. (1974) *ibid.*, pp. 143–168.

[2] Pratt, J. B. (1928) *The Pilgrimage of Buddhism*, Macmillan, London.

the sense of being means of procuring anything from him. Their value is subjective purely. A prayer for peace or purity is likely to bring about its own fulfillment, especially if accompanied by the thought of the Buddha as our ideal. The Buddha, indeed, is for practical purposes quite dead, but he is the ideal of what humanity might be and of what each of us ought to be. Thus prayer for the enlightened Buddhist is not supplication but mental discipline.' . . .

But there is a third theory or prayer, which, since it is something of a compromise between the subjective and objective views, is perhaps the commonest of all. This universe is governed primarily by the moral law of justice or Karma. Merit can never fail to produce good results. Now though the Buddha cannot—or at any rate does not—hear and answer prayer, it is still true that the repetition of the Buddha's words with reverence and a pure heart are infallible means of acquiring merit and cannot lose their reward. The thing works automatically. Thus your father is ill. You do not make a petitional prayer to the Buddha for his recovery. But you chant sacred Pali verses, or get the holy monks to do so for you, with the mental intention that the merit thus acquired shall be applied to your father's account. It will not infallibly restore his health any more than in Christian theory a prayer to God would do so. But it will infallibly tend to do so; and even if his (or your) evil Karma be so great that he dies just the same, your prayer cannot be of no effect, for it will have counterbalanced some of the evil Karma which he or you have acquired.

(Pratt, J. B. (1928) *ibid*, pp. 134–135.)


PLEASE PAUSE HERE
DO NOT READ ON UNTIL YOU HAVE COMPLETED THE EXERCISE


### 4.2.2.7 Specimen answer
The three motives are: to ask for the Buddha's assistance for concrete necessities; to obtain a feeling of peace and purification through a 'spiritual' exercise; to acquire in accordance with the law of karma, a good record which will help towards a good reincarnation. This motivation may differ in different people. An individual may be moved by more than one such motive.

---

4.2.2.8 *Orthodox* Buddhism in Sri Lanka is clearly based on the Sangha; it is difficult to estimate its numerical strength, for monastic vows are often only temporary. Approximate statistics speak of 3,000 monasteries (varying greatly in size), of about 20,000 ordained monks, and almost as many young aspirants in training. These monks are distributed in three groups (*nikāyas*). The Siamese group, founded in 1740, is thus called because its founders derived their ordination and their customs from Siam. By virtue of an old royal decree this group only accepts candidates from the highest caste. The other two groups, Amarapura and Ramanya, founded in 1803 and 1835, are more faithful to the Founder's teaching on this point and accept people from all classes. The Ramanya is the strictest in its observances; in it the vow of poverty is strictly adhered to and popular devotional practices are rejected. The leaders of these three groups are sovereign in their own sphere and independent of each other.

4.2.2.9 In Ceylonese tradition the centre of general and monastic training is called the *Pirivena*. Buddhism has depended greatly on the educational influence of the Pirivenas. This influence persists but it has lost its original ascetic vigour. Monastic liturgies continue; these include the chanting of sacred texts in the morning and the evening, and the two sessions of 'public confession' (*pātimokkha*) each month. There is a cycle of annual observances, such as those marking the beginning and the end of the rainy season, which are times when special recollection is enjoined. For the people the monastic shrines offer many ceremonies, occurring both at regular times and on occasions. There are the gift-offerings of rice, of incense and of flowers to the Buddha; there is exorcism of places or persons under evil spells, which is effected by chants and recitation of sacred texts; there are processions in the monasteries or in the towns, like the famous procession of the Buddha's Tooth, preserved in the great temple of Kandy; more generally, there is welcome and counsel by the monks for those who come to seek their help.

4.2.2.10 Besides the maintenance of traditional customs there has been, since the end of the last century an effort of renewal. At the origins of this movement was an American, Colonel H. S. Olcott, author of a famous 'Buddhist Catechism' and, more influential still, D. D. Hewavitarane (1864–1944) whose monastic name was Anagārika Dharmapāla. The latter founded the Mahabodhi Siciety and a number of periodicals, as well as making numerous appeals for a return to Buddhism and to the authentic spirit of Ceylon. The present-day promoters of this revival celebrated with great pomp the 2500th anniversary of the birth of the Buddha (Buddha-Jayanti) in 1956. They have launched a series of scholarly works as well as a general programme of 'Buddhification' of their country (often demonstrating their hostility to other religions, Hinduism, Islam and, above all, Christianity). Various forms of social and youth work have also been undertaken. Independence has increased both the enthusiasm and the resources of the revivalists.

4.2.2.11 Thus Buddhism remains the strongest spiritual force in Sri Lanka. It is supported by a government which is itself largely Buddhist and reaches out to the population through a vast network of educational activities and the mass media. Although Buddhism takes many forms amongst the people of Ceylon because of its basic flexibility, its essential unity is not threatened.

## 4.3 China: Buddhism dispossessed

### 4.3.1 Historical background

4.3.1.1 According to tradition, the first Buddhist missionaries in China were two monks who had been met by imperial ambassadors in Central Asia and taken to the Emperor Ming-Ti in 62 CE. Once again we see that it was a monarch who made the initial contact. It was another monarch, the Tartar ruler of a northern state, Shih Chi-Lung, who was the first to allow the Chinese to become monks in about 360 CE. Similarly, in 520, a decisive stage was reached when a famous Indian monk, Bodhidharma, was received at the imperial court at Nankin by a ruler who was already a Buddhist. There seems at this point to have been a close bond between the Sangha and the State. (Further details of the history of Buddhism in China are given by Robinson, *Encyclopedia*, pp. 319–23, and by *Ling*, §§4.36, 4.37, 5.20, 5.21 and 6.47.)

4.3.1.2 Nevertheless, Buddhism, the champion of individualism and of progress through change, was resisted by conservative Confucianism which had, until then, shaped the attitude of the governing powers. Buddhism, however, continued to expand, if not at the expense of Confucianism, at least alongside it. But at the end of the Sung dynasty in the ninth century Confucianism regained the upper hand. Then the Ming dynasty and the Manchus showed themselves to be suspicious of a doctrine which encouraged abandonment of the world and the disruption of normal social relations. In their eyes there was a real risk that this would lead to an undermining of the values of the State and the availability of citizens to serve it. They blocked the further expansion of Buddhism and often actually reduced the real influence of the monks. From that time onwards, although Buddhism has been tolerated as an historic reality, it has continued to lose its influence and its vitality in China.

## 4.3.2 The first half of the twentieth century

4.3.2.1 During this period (China has been a Republic since 1911) one must note the different religious attitudes in different circles of Chinese Buddhism.

As far as the monks were concerned, on the one hand there was a continuation of the contemplative endeavour, by withdrawal from worldly interests, in accordance with the precepts of the Ch'an school; on the other some bhikkhus sought to imitate in the religious sphere the general movement of national renewal begun by the Republic and stimulated by the infiltration of Marxist ideas amongst intellectuals from about 1920. Movements arose at this time which had as their objective: 'to defend the religion, propagate the faith, reform the order and promote education' (manifesto quoted in *Ling*, §7.42).

4.3.2.2 At a more popular level, among the monks but principally among the laity, there was a revival of the devotional movement of the Pure Land and of the cult of Amito; by this path several groups earnestly sought profound spiritual experience by restoring the inner meaning to external practices.

4.3.2.3 As for the position of the people in general, the situation is very complex. In practice China has had three religions, or more precisely three great philosophical-ethical-religious systems: Confucianism, Taoism and Buddhism. But, as we noted earlier, there is a common proverb which says: 'Three religions, one religion'. In fact it is true that the people had recourse to all three according to different circumstances. Funeral rites and the cult of respect rendered to the dead could be connected with Buddhism because of its preaching on the subject of the fragility of life and of the chain of reincarnation with all its risks of ill outcome. Confucianism continued, to a considerable extent, to inspire the public life of the State and the conduct of its administrators. Taoism, derived from an esoteric philosophy, provided colourful rituals for the people, which were not without magical value in their estimation. Such rituals were considered useful in everyday life for the avoidance of misfortune and the assurance of success in this world or in the world beyond. (On the subject of Confucianism refer to the article by A. C. Graham in the *Encyclopedia*, pp. 357–73; on Taoism, see Eichorn's article, *Encyclopedia*, pp. 374–92.)

4.3.2.4 In particular the funerary activity of Chinese Buddhism was based on the belief that the departed could not be certain that their own merits were enough to avert a sorrowful rebirth (perhaps even in hell). But the sacred texts recited or sung by a group of monks after a death would avert this danger.

4.3.2.5 Devout Buddhist layfolk would frequently go to the temples (see §4.3.2.8 below). Families who were most regular in their observance would also attend, at least on occasion, the monastic offices at the beginning and the middle of each lunar month and at certain feasts. Nevertheless it is at home that devout Buddhists especially render devotion to the *Fo* (Buddhas) and the *P'usa* (Bodhisattvas); usually Amito and Kwan-Yin. This domestic cult consists mainly of the recitation of sūtras (sacred texts), of the repetition of the formula *Namo O-mi-to Fo*, or 'adoration to the Buddha Amito'; and of petitions to various P'usa, above all to Kwan-Yin.

### 4.3.2.6 Exercise

To remind yourself what a Bodhisattva (Chinese: P'usa) is, look back at §§3.2.2.3–3.2.2.7 above, where Kwan-Yin was mentioned. Then read the following passage by Pratt, which, although rather long, is very characteristic. As you read, consider these questions to answer afterwards: What is one to think of Kwan-Yin? Is he or she a real figure? To what essential aspect of Buddhism may this figure be related? (Refer also to *Encyclopedia*, p. 314.)

> Kwan-Yin is, as I have said, the Chinese form of Avalokitesvara, the great Bodhisattva of mercy. In becoming a Chinese P'usa, however, the Bodhisattva underwent a number of changes, the most notable of which, perhaps, was the transformation of his sex. Though sometimes presented as a male, Kwan-Yin is usually represented and almost invariably thought of as distinctly a woman. She is known universally as the Goddess of Mercy. It was doubtless the longing of the human heart for something motherly in the divine that was the ultimate cause of this transformation. . . . Kwan-Yin is the loving mother of all the needy. She watches over those in danger and listens to the prayers of all who suffer or are frightened. She gives children to the childless, and probably is the recipient of more earnest prayers than all the rest of the Buddhist cycle combined. The Chinese have adopted her to a unique degree. They will have it that she once lived in China, as a Chinese. . .
>
> Her father, the king, wished her to marry but she refused and escaped to the White Sparrow Convent, where the nuns put her in the kitchen. The King, enraged at her departure, sent his troops to burn the convent, but Kwan-Yin prayed, and in answer to her prayer a heavy rain extinguished the flames. Her father, however, had her brought back to the palace, and gave her the choice between marriage and death. The little saint replied that she preferred death. She was tortured, but refused to change her choice, and was at length strangled; a local god in the form of a tiger seized her body and disappeared with it into the forest. She herself descended into hell, whereupon hell became a paradise, with gardens of lilies—so lovely a place as to be entirely useless in the judicial system of the universe. In fact, Yen-lo, the king of hell, had to beg her to depart. On her return from hell the Buddha appeared to her and gave her a shining pearl, and advised her to retire to the island of P'uto, off the coast of Chekiang. Some say she was carried thither by a god, some that she floated there on a water lily, while a third account, popular on the island itself, insists that she was born (or born again) on a rocky islet just off from P'uto, connected with it by a short bridge. . . . At any rate, the island of P'uto has been

her peculiar home for hundreds of years, and numberless are the pilgrims who travel there, season after season, in picturesque junks with brown sails and high poop, and a fish's eye painted on the prow.

The little lady Kwan-Yin is one of the loveliest forms of Buddhist mythology. She has not a trait one could wish absent or altered.

(Pratt, J. B. (1928) *ibid.*, pp. 296–297.)

Now write your answers to the questions posed above.


### PLEASE PAUSE HERE
DO NOT READ ON UNTIL YOU HAVE COMPLETED THE EXERCISE


### 4.3.2.7 Specimen answer

It all depends on the sense that is given to the world *real..* . . . Kwan-Yin was originally a mythical invention, but she certainly corresponds to an essential aspect of Buddhism—the comparison of the Enlightened Ones for human misery. Many Buddhists, both in the present and in the past, show in their lives that they possess this compassion in a high degree. It is possible to understand how the people might have identified a person of such virtue with Kwan-Yin.

---

4.3.2.8 Devout Chinese Buddhists cherished aspirations both for this life and for the future state. In this life they sought the maintenance of peace, both private and public, preservation from disaster and the achievement of success in their careers. As for future existence, it is naturally desired that this will be happy. Even though Buddhist doctrine and the most orthodox monks deny it, on the grounds that the future of a person is determined by the Karma that he has accumulated, the people believe that prayer can be in some sense efficacious. R. H. Robinson writes: 'It is hard to say whether Chinese Buddhists "pray" without misleading the reader' (*Encyclopedia*, p. 327). It may help to see what he means to read the following passage.

> The worship of the Chinese layman in the temple is chiefly individual worship. Sometimes, indeed, he is present at the chanting servce of the monks. This is often a mere chance coincidence, and not an unusual one, since (as we have seen) the monks have two or three services every day. In some devout Buddhist families, however, it is not a matter of chance; for the more strict families observe the custom of attending the early morning service in a near-by monastery or convent on the first and fifteenth of every moon. On these occasions they first listen to the chanting of the monks—or of the nuns—and after these have finished, the family, with the father at their head, repeats a certain ritual of prayer and praise before the Buddha . . . This family service is usually held about four in the morning . . . Most Buddhist families attend the services on behalf of their own dead, and those held on special occasions, and beyond that it is only now and then that they visit a temple . . .
>
> As a rule, when a Chinese Buddhist goes to his temple it is not to hear a sermon nor to listen while someone else prays. He goes there to pray himself. Communal worship is something of which the Chinese have

very little conception. It is odd how difficult it seems to be for Westerners to grasp this fact, even when they have resided for some time in China. . . . The laymen who do come to the temple to pray do so in part because of the opportunity here at hand to make offerings to the Fos and P'usas—both of gifts for the immediate glorification of the Holy Ones, and also of money to aid in support of the Sangha. By these means one acquires merit. Another reason for worship in the temple is that the sacred associations of the place and the presence of the images makes one feel more like praying—puts one in a more religious frame of mind—and presumably the prayer in such circumstances is worth more. Probably the most ignorant directly worship the temple images (whatever that may mean!), but for most laymen the image seems to be merely a sacred representation of the holy Being, who himself is in heaven.

(Pratt, J. B. (1928), *ibid.*, pp. 358–359.)

### 4.3.2.9 Question

Now refer back to our discussion of the motives of 'prayer' in the section on Buddhism in Sri Lanka (§4.2.2.6 above). Compare the motives described in that passage with those suggested in the passages you have just read. Are the motives the same, or are there special features of 'prayer' in Chinese Buddhism?

PLEASE PAUSE HERE

DO NOT READ ON UNTIL YOU HAVE COMPLETED THE EXERCISE

### 4.3.2.10 Specimen answer and discussion

The motives indicated in the passages just cited are: psychological stimulation, the acquisition of merit, belief in the assistance of the Buddha who 'hears' prayers. These motives correspond to those described above in §4.2.2.6, and are essentially the same in all the popular forms of Buddhism among the masses. It is impossible to say in what proportion these motives are combined in any particular case. Obviously one can expect a greater influence of the third motive in the pietist groups in China who believe in Amito, Kwan-Yin and the 'Pure Land' than in the meditative sects relying on individual personal effort. According to the obscure yet deeply-felt sentiments of many of the faithful it is, in a mysterious sense, *to the Buddha himself that their prayer is really directed*. Some would say that this is merely a mental remembrance of the Buddha as a past figure, which has a present psychological effect. However, in many cases it would seem that there is the desire for, if not the conviction of, an actual presence of the Buddha and the feeling that prayers to him are answered.

---

4.3.2.11 The forms of Chinese Buddhist devotion were very varied and often picturesque—as may be seen from the following description, which relates to customs in the late 1920s:

The devout Buddhist layman—and more especially the devout Buddhist laywoman—goes to the temple from time to time to pray and make her vows, to gain assistance, acquire merit, and also to get, if possible, a glimpse into the future. For fortune-telling is inextricably mixed up with worship in most Chinese temples which are popular with the masses. . .

Worship is not always followed by fortune-telling, and in fact the majority of worshippers simply come in, present an offering of incense, candles, paper money, flowers or vegetables, make their prayers and depart, without seeking to unveil the future. I remember a typical scene in a temple in Swatow—the temple swarming with earnest worshippers, mostly women and girls, kneeling with lighted incense sticks, bowing deeply before the draped image, and moving their lips in prayer. Many offered large leaves of gilt paper money. After presenting them with bows before the altar they would put them in a kind of incinerator, provided for the purpose.

(Pratt, J. B. (1928) *ibid.*, pp. 354–345.)

4.3.2.12 What do you think of this description? Are such practices really Buddhist at all, compared with what you know about the time-honoured doctrines and practices of mainstream Buddhism?

---

*An answer:* I have already remarked several times that to 'basic' Buddhism as it was described in the second part of these units, all kinds of additions have been made. All kinds of practices have been tolerated, whether derived from pre-existing beliefs or from the needs and the simple piety of the less instructed faithful. The latter especially have looked to Buddhism for security or success in this world, which the monastic élite regard as worthy of contempt (even though they get their subsistence from the fruits of it!) The Founder himself had already tolerated such an attitude for beginners in the monastic life, and more generally for well-intentioned folk who remained in secular life. His successors have done the same.

4.3.2.13 It must be recognized that in the face of such popular customs the efforts of renewal in Chinese Buddhism, to which reference was made above (§4.3.2.1), did not succeed in bringing about a large-scale transformation Here are the criticisms made by a zealous Chinese reformer, T'ai Hsu[1] about 1930:

In China the Buddhists have the following shortcomings: First, they are seldom interested in social service or the work of educating the society. The priests or rather monks are generally ignorant, and their services to society are confined to singing of masses or prayers in the funeral services. Secondly, although the monks divide themselves into sects or schools, each pursuing a special object, yet they always fail to accomplish that object. Thirdly, the monks are always religious recluses, taking no interest in the affairs of the community or the country and they are in turn slighted by the Government or the ruling classes. Fourthly, most of the Chinese Buddhist monks lack the necessary modern scientific knowledge and are also ignorant of the current thoughts and ideas in the world. In view of such disabilities, they are unable to preach the doctrines of the Buddha in such a way as to

[1] Hsu, T'ai (1930) 'A statement to Asiatic Buddhists', in *The Young East*, Vol. I, pp. 179–180.

appeal to the minds of the modern people. The Chinese Buddhist monks, however, have also their good points:

1  Most of the devout monks always lead a most austere life of a religious recluse. They remain in inaccessible regions, leave all the vanity and human desires behind and devote themselves exclusively to prayer and contemplation.

2  Although the monks divide themselves into different sects or schools, yet their views are liberal and tolerant. They never engage themselves in religious controversies.

3  The Chinese monks are internationalists. They regard the human society in the world as of the same family regardless of races, creeds, or nationalities. This is the fundamental principle on which the Buddha founded his teachings.

4  Although the thoughts and religious notions of the Buddhist monks in China have somewhat undergone a change during the Sui and T'ang dynasties, yet up to the present they still preserve the main features of primitive Buddhism.

### 4.3.2.14  Exercise

Now write some comments on the passage. Does it strike you as a fair criticism? What points can you note either in favour of or against the author's judgement. (Read the account of T'ai Hsu's reforming efforts in *Encyclopedia*, pp. 335–6.)

### PLEASE PAUSE HERE
#### DO NOT READ ON UNTIL YOU HAVE COMPLETED THE EXERCISE

### 4.3.2.15  Specimen answer and discussion

It must be remembered that the author was a reformer and that his text is a manifesto in which everything is simplified and sharply delineated. I would suggest an answer to the questions we have put along the following lines. The qualities of austerity, of tolerance and of goodwill are certainly characteristics of Buddhist life. The degree of ignorance (or knowledge) of Chinese monks at the beginning of the century cannot be easily measured; it seems certain, however, that many of them merited T'ai Hsu's criticism. Moreover one must allow what he says concerning their separation from the mass of the people. On the other hand one must not forget that an ideal of peace and self-denial, and more especially the example of these qualities, may be an important positive contribution to the progress of a people.

### 4.3.3  Buddhism in process of elimination

Such then is a picture of Chinese Buddhism, already under pressure, with numerous and diverse accretions, but still rooted in tradition, which was to be confronted with the Mao's victorious Communism after 1949. (For a fuller treatment of this subject, I recommend the three volumes by H. Welch cited in the bibliography, and particularly the third).[1]

[1] Welch, H. (1967) *The Practice of Chinese Buddhism 1900–1950*, Harvard University Press; (1968) *The Buddhist Revival in China*, Harvard University Press; (1972) *Buddhism under Mao*, Harvard University Press.

4.3.3.1 Until 1966, in principle, the new government's policy was to proclaim freedom of religion (at least for Chinese religions—the same was not true of foreign or 'imperialist' religions). This was set out in Article 5 of the Common Programme of the Party, of 20 September 1949. It was made clear, however, that even if the religions were not obliged to manifest 'ideological conformity' they did have to demonstrate 'political conformity' in their ideas, their conduct, their activities. This was a distinction made by Chou En Lai as early as 5 May 1950.[1] According to theory the revolutionary process of economic and social liberation and of the education of the people is the first priority and will quickly in itself lead to a total elimination of religion.

4.3.3.2 This hope of the leaders did not prevent certain zealous activitists inspired by various of Mao's writings from beginning immediately in some areas a physical struggle against Buddhism, its institutions and its members. But the government expressed its disapproval and calmed the activists. The government preferred to set up centralizing bodies to promote 'reformation'. For religious purposes there was, for example, the *Chinese Buddhist Association*; for administrative purposes there was the *Religious Affairs Bureau*, which was to follow a progressive overall plan of 'reform'.

4.3.3.3 *The law of agrarian reform* specifies that 'the rural land belonging to ancestral shrines, temples, monasteries, churches, schools and organizations shall be requisitioned'. The same law provides that 'monks, nuns, and Taoist priests should be given shares of land and other means of production equal to those of the peasants if they have no other means of making a living and are able and willing to engage in agricultural work'. But many monks were incapable of fulfilling this last condition and the land allocated to the monastic communities was reduced by a corresponding amount. Many monasteries were thus reduced to poverty or simply eliminated. Others were absorbed into rural co-operatives.

4.3.3.4 Monks in the towns were only able to keep their residences on condition that they undertook productive work, such as textile weaving, or manufacture of bags made from jute. Their success in such activities was rare and limited. Moreover, with a few exceptions, their former sources of income had dried up; there were no more gifts from the pious laity, no more fees for funerals and other ceremonies, no more rents from properties which were now confiscated. The monastic system was also undermined from within. Some superiors were harassed or imprisoned because of resistance or 'incapacity'. After a few years 90 per cent of the monks seem to have withdrawn from their monastic vocation. The laity had still fewer reasons to attach themselves to something which seemed very much a thing of the past and to have been overtaken by events.

4.3.3.5 All this clearing away of the old structures has provided the framework for a *psychological reform*. The aim is to make Buddhists and particularly monks (who are presented as former property owners, conservative and selfish in outlook) into collectivized citizens, devoted, without personal consideration, to the common good. This means, in practice, that they should be dedicated to the development of the country through productive contribution as workers. This new mentality must be acquired through methodical study, in class meetings and intensive discussion groups. This mentality is expected to be expressed in deeds, which may even take the form of enrolment in the army—despite the previous monastic

---

[1] Welch, H. (1972) *ibid.*, p. 3.

profession of non-violence. To take part in intense and time-demanding public work is only possible if Buddhist studies and ceremonies are greatly reduced or suppressed.

4.3.3.6 In order to understand the problem more clearly two things should be borne in mind. As I pointed out earlier when discussing the monastic life, the Buddhist monk is not bound by perpetual vows. He may without any disgrace end his monastic commitment if he considers it better or inevitable to do so. Also, as Welch says:

> We should try to see the Communists' reform of the monastic system in the perspective of history. Attacks on the Sangha for parasitism were as old as the Mahāyāna in China. Control of the Sangha, either aimed at purifying it or preventing sedition, was also nothing new.
> (Welch, H. (1972) *ibid*, p. 139)

Here we find once more the relationship between the Community and the State, already noted with reference to Sri Lanka, but in this case acting *against* the interests of the Sangha, seeking to bring it into line (and to bring about its gradual elimination).

4.3.3.7 It was against this backcloth that the Cultural Revolution occurred.[1] Here we can only summarize the situation. Temples, associations, newspapers, Buddhist gatherings, even the Bureau of Religious Affairs (henceforth considered to be useless) were all swept away. It is no exaggeration to say that the Buddhist Sangha, as a nation-wide community, disappeared. Some culturally important monasteries survive as museums with monks as keepers. Internationally, for the benefit of world opinion and foreign Buddhists, freedom of religion is still proclaimed. But Buddhist doctrine itself must support official doctrine or disappear. The vigilant and challenging role played by Buddhism in Ceylon is obviously impossible.

4.3.3.8 As for what is happening, what has disappeared, or what has survived at a deeper level, as for what will happen in the China of the future, Welch writes:

> When people are suddenly cut off from the customs through which their lives have been kept in balance over many centuries, when the behavioural ecology, so to speak, is upset, the results cannot be foreseen. I believe that people have certain psychological needs—religious needs—which the Communist Party cannot fill.
> (Welch, H. (1972) *ibid.*, p. 385)

But futurology is not part of this present course . . .

Read what Robinson says about the lot of Buddhism under Chinese Communism (*Encyclopedia*, pp. 336–7). Comment on his statement:

> The Chinese Communists are not destroying the cultural appurtenances of Buddhism, but they are cutting at the economic roots of the Sangha, and preventing the monks from carrying out the functions of the homeless life. The survival of Buddhism in mainland China depends on a liberalization of the regime within the next two decades.

[1] Welch, H. (1972), *ibid.*, p. 361–371.

These words were written in 1959. Do they seem to be justified by events since then?

---

An answer is not easy to give. The last three points of the quotation seem to be clearly appropriate, but the first seems too optimistic. The Cultural Revolution took place later and explains the more serious interpretation given in Welch's book which was written in the light of those events. Today the picture is still unclear.

## 4.4 Japan: Buddhism 'disestablished' but respected

### 4.4.1 Historical background

4.4.1.1 From the time of its introduction into Japan Buddhism was involved in the rivalries of powerful rulers. Prince Shotoku (574–621 CE), Regent of the Empire for thirty years, had proclaimed Buddhism as the State religion. During his reign Buddhism was, in the main, a preserve of the 'progressive' aristocracy. It 'became virtually a State-Church, with the ruler protecting, encouraging and supporting the work of the monks, and the monks willingly giving their allegiance and support to the ruler'. (*Ling*, §5.24; for the early history of Buddhism in Japan, and later developments, see *Ling*, §§5.25, 5.28, 6.28 and *Encyclopedia*, pp. 337–341.)

4.4.1.2 At that time, one Buddhist text in particular acquired great renown in Japan; it was the Saddharmapundarikasūtra (in Japanese, *Hokke-kyo*). It recommended devotion to two figures whom we have already encountered in our study—the Buddha Amita (in Japanese Amida) and the Bodhisattva Avalokitesvara (the Chinese Kwan-Yin; in Japanese, Kwannon; see §3.2.2.6 above). Both the text and the devotional practices associated with it had reached Japan after first crossing China. On the other hand there were texts which pointed in a different direction—towards independent contemplation of a non-theistic kind. Two schools, Jōdō and Zen, reflected respectively these two recurring tendencies in man's religious quest; one preaching salvation through Another (*tariki*), the other salvation through oneself (*jiriki*) (see §3.2.2.10 above).

4.4.1.3 Salvation through Another was greatly favoured among the people. The pioneer of this 'way' in Japan, the monk Hōnen (see §3.2.2.8d above), has left his own account of how, after attempts at salvation through his own endeavours, he arrived at a 'trusting faith' in Amida. The Zendo whom Hōnen refers to in the following text was a great Chinese master who and preached the necessity of faith in and invocation of Amida, and the hope of being consequently reborn in the 'Paradise of the West', the 'Pure Land'. (More particulars about the fascinating sage Hōnen are to be found in the *Encyclopedia*, pp. 339–40.) Here then are Hōnen's words:[1]

> Having a deep desire to obtain salvation and with faith in the teaching of the various scriptures, I practised many forms of self discipline. . . .

---

[1] From Coates, H. and Ishizuka (eds) (1930) *Hōnen, The Buddhist Saint*, Tokyo. This book contains several texts of the same kind.

But the fact is I do not keep even the precepts, nor do I attain to any one of the many forms of meditation. . . . Unless one get free from evil conduct and evil passion how shall he obtain deliverance from the bondage of birth and death? Alas! alas! What shall I do? What shall I do? The like of us are incompetent to practise the three disciplines of the precepts, meditations, and knowledge. And so I inquired of a great many learned men and priests whether there is any other way of salvation than these disciplines, but no one could either teach me the way or even suggest it. At last I went into the library where all the Scriptures were, all by myself, and with a heavy heart read them all through. I hit upon a passage in Zendo's Commentary, which runs as follows: 'Only repeat the name of Amitabha with all your heart, whether walking or standing, whether sitting or lying: never cease the practice of it for a moment. 'This is the very work which unfailingly issues in salvation; for it is in accordance with the Original Vow of Amida Buddha.'

In order to understand more deeply this devotional attitude in some forms of Japanese Buddhism, we may add to the passage just quoted from Hōnen the following modern text by Kosho Otani,[1] the recent patriarch of one of the great divisions (Shin) of this movement:

How can we find true salvation? How can we solve this problem (the problem of human passions)? Man, whose knowledge is limited, cannot produce a satisfactory answer to this problem. We can never discover by pure intellectual knowledge a way to wipe out all afflictions. Of course, in ordinary daily life money, medicine, or good deeds may solve immediate problems. But the fundamental suffering and anxiety of human existence cannot be eliminated by our feeble activities. Man is quite helpless and incapable of resolving the problems of existence through his own power. Man is filled with passions and desires which becloud his insight and restrain his efforts. Only in the power of the Buddha which transcends man is there to be found salvation. . . . Just as a babe must be tended by its mother, so we too gain salvation through the compassion of the Buddha of Infinite Mercy. Because the Buddha presents eternal life to us, his compassion is the foundation upon which we can build a noble life. . . . This power [scil. the power of the Main Vow of Amida] which transcends all relative and limited things is eternal and unlimited, and because by it all limited things are saved, it is called salvation by a power outside of them. . . . The faith which looks up to the benevolence of the Buddha becomes a fountainhead of power for living the good life. Though we live in an existence filled with suffering and passion, yet in the power of our faith that we live in Buddha's mercy and compassion, we find hope, strength and encouragement.

(Otani, K. (1957) *Ibid*, pp. 14–15)

### 4.4.1.5 Exercise
After reading those two passages, from Hōnen and from Kosho Otani, compare the doctrinal standpoint expressed in them with the basic assumptions of monotheistic religions, such as Judaism, Christianity and Islam. These religions acknowledge the existence of a Supreme Being who is

[1]Otani, K. (1957) *Sermons on Shin Buddhism.*

omnipotent and merciful, and who can be called upon to give succour. Do you recognize a similar outlook in the two passages just quoted? Do these two expressions of religious belief seem to you to be truly 'theistic'? Or are there significant differences between such apparently 'theistic' views and the basic belief of the monotheistic religions mentioned? Write your comments in your notebook.

**PLEASE PAUSE HERE**

DO NOT READ ON UNTIL YOU HAVE COMPLETED THE EXERCISE

### 4.4.1.6 Specimen answer and discussion

No doubt your immediate reaction will have been to notice similarities. Amida occupies more or less the same position as God in Christianity or Islam. The descriptions of the Paradises of the West as places of delight have something in common with the description of paradises in the Qu'ran. Buddhist invocation makes one think of certain forms of Christian and Muslim prayer. Nevertheless there is one absolutely capital distinction. In Christianity and Islam, believing in God, going to fellowship with God in an afterlife, and existing with him there in a mysterious state, is the ultimate form of salvation, the final happiness. In Buddhism, on the other hand, the 'theistic' devotion and practices of piety are provisional. They remain imperfect and must be surpassed. The final state of Nirvāna is situated 'beyond' prayer, beyond paradises and beyond 'God' himself—beyond any 'personalization' however lofty.

---

4.4.1.7. In Japan, as elsewhere, Buddhism rested (with all the advantages and dangers that this implies) on the three-cornered base: monastic Sangha, political power and popular support from a population who, inclined towards ritualism and syncretism, mingled new trends with ancient beliefs. Although Buddhism in Japan was at first primarily the religion of the aristocracy, there was an official policy of spreading it to the people. The peaceful and tolerant nature of Buddhism could accommodate within it earlier rites and beliefs which had preceded it in Japan.

4.4.1.8 In your *Encyclopedia* (pp. 342–56) there is an article by G. Bowness on Shintō, the Japanese religion which honoured higher, invisible beings from whom, it was believed, the Emperor was descended. Shintō and Buddhism combined very well, to such an extent that temples were erected for the use of the two religions jointly. Buddhism remained the more influential. It was more structured and more protected, more highly developed in its ideas, its rituals and its buildings. But the message and success of Buddhism was not regarded in any way as an attack on Shintō, since Buddhism had no destructive animus against other religions. A willingness to be accommodating in religion was a characteristic of Japan in general throughout its history. Partly this stemmed from the practical consideration that: 'two protections and two precautions are better than one'. The government shared this popular sentiment. Before erecting the gigantic statue of the Buddha at Nara, which still stands today, the Emperor Shomu wished to be certain of the consent of the traditional, pre-Buddhist deities. He sent the famous monk Gyōgi to the temple of the Sun goddess, the centre of the Shintō cult. The goddess's reply was that the Buddha Vairocana (in Japanese, Dainichi) was only a form of herself; everything was all right! (See *Encyclopedia*, p. 351.)

4.4.1.9 In line with this process of identification, the various Shintō deities were regarded in the same way as the Hindu deities had been in India: that is, as inferior personages emanating in some sense from the Buddha, who was considered to be the supreme reality. Similar accommodations were to be found in matters of ritual. The first Buddhist 'text' printed in Japan, on the orders of an Empress in 770 CE, was a formula or charm-spell in Sanskrit, transliterated into Chinese characters. A million copies were imprinted.

**4.4.1.10 Exercise**

Basing your answer on what you have read about the expansion and development of Buddhism in the Far East, write a brief summary of the factors which led to the great success of Buddhism in Japan.

PLEASE PAUSE HERE
DO NOT READ ON UNTIL YOU HAVE COMPLETED THE EXERCISE

**4.4.1.11 Specimen answer and discussion**

The rapid importation of ideas and arts from China had an immense effect on Japan and on the fortunes of Buddhism there. In 709, Nara was made the capital and became a large metropolis, embellished with the new culture and religion. This was due also to the advent in large numbers of Korean and Chinese scholars, who developed a flourishing monastic culture and schools of philosophy.

Chinese culture, including its religious aspects, was considered as the model to be followed by all the peoples of East Asia, and especially by Japan. Buddhism, already 1000 years old, with its systematically developed doctrines, constituted a much stronger reality than Shintō which was a 'nature-religion' and mythology of a fairly elementary kind. The Buddhist masters were not only learned in doctrine, but in literature, the arts and philosophy. On this account they enjoyed very considerable prestige which aided their propaganda. The Buddhists knew how to adapt themselves to the inclinations of the sovereign and of the governing élite. Among these, two categories of converts were of particular importance—the 'progressive' intellectuals and pious aristocratic ladies. As far as the people were concerned, Buddhism demonstrated its usual tolerance, supplying gods, heavens, hells, and rituals, which were in some respects magical but in any event impressive. J. Murdoch[1] made the following remarks which are relevant to our present question:

> To Shōtoku Taishi Buddhism was evidently a religion of the rational moral sense—a religion not only of obligation or of fear but of gratitude for the receipt of blessings, if not unsought for at least undeserved. But to most of his contemporaries, Buddhism was simply a splendidly easy device for obtaining temporal and perhaps everlasting prosperity, for dodging the Devil or Devils, and escaping the pains and penalties of the various Hells. . . . Buddhism made its appeal to the ignorant vulgar by its magicians and exorcists, by its living saints in the flesh who were supposed to possess strong court interest with the dignitaries of the ghostly world, by the gorgeousness of its temples and the solemn pomp

[1] Murdoch, J. (1910) *A History of Japan*, Vol. 1, pp. 174–5, Asiatic Society of Japan, London.

of its ritual observances. Yet in spite of all this it held in its embrace higher and loftier elements that could do, and did do, much for the culture and civilization of Japan.

---

The history of the following centuries—the 'Buddhist centuries' of Japan—is too complex to be recounted here. Reference should be made to the sections in *Ling* indicated above in §4.4.1.1. Certain facts stand out. The close liaison between the monastic Community and the State continued to the extent that the monasteries, their dependents and their wealth even became involved in military conflicts. Sometimes these interventions turned out badly. if the side supported by the monks lost, then the victorious adversary would exact revenge, holding to ransom, beseiging, or even destroying the monasteries. In 1574 the Shōgun Nobunaga took the Hiei-San monastery of the Tendai sect by storm, burning, it is said, 3,000 residences and temples and having almost all the monks put to death either in the flames or by the sword.

4.4.1.12 From the 1660s onwards the Tokugawa shōguns whilst protecting the religious and cultural life of Buddhism, were at the same time anxious to control it. One of the methods of control, indirect but effective, was the admission into Japan, particularly into the court and the aristocracy, of two other rival ideologies: namely the Christian religion through Western missionaries and Confucianism through Chinese scholars and intellectual influence. As Pratt[1] says 'Confucian scholars quite wrested the intellectual and moral leadership of the land from the Buddhists, and the upper classes ceased to be interested in Buddhism'.

4.4.1.13 About the beginning of the nineteenth century, a new adversary replaced Christianity, which had been proscribed since the end of the sixteenth century CE. This variant of Shintō was supported by intellectuals and by the military, who opposed both the religious privileges of Buddhism and the political domination of the Tokugawa regime 1603–1867). The restoration of Imperial power in 1868 and the beginning of the 'Era of Enlightened Government' (Meiji) struck a hard blow at Buddhism, which ceased to be the State religion and thus lost one of the three pillars of its support. Its place of honour was now taken by Shintō, with its belief in the sacred character of the Emperor and of the nation itself. Moreover, the country was opened again to Christian missionaries and Western traders—these latter providing an example of material acquisitiveness and desires very different from the message of Buddhism.

4.4.1.14 These traumatic changes could have destroyed Buddhism in Japan; in reality they liberated it from a liaison with the State and the world which had begun to crush it and to endanger Buddhist spiritual detachment. They also led to a revival which involved the best elements in Buddhism in the scholarly study of doctrine and in social work amongst the people. A remaining encumbrance, which continued to weigh heavily upon Japanese Buddhism, was its vast possessions in land and its financial power generally. The monasteries were often, although not always, very wealthy. The Second World War destroyed thousands of sanctuaries and monasteries both great and small. The agrarian reforms, and the compulsory redistribution of the land carried out by the government at the suggestion of the Americans, took away large areas of land from the monasteries, reducing some of them to poverty.

---

[1] Pratt, J. B. (1928) *op. cit.*, p. 493.

Buddhism, like all religions in our own age, also underwent a new searching test—the criticism of secularists and of non-believing humanists, whether Marxists or not. In consequence, the allegiance of many of its members, already weakened by other factors, was lost.

### 4.4.2 The present-day situation

How has Japanese Buddhism weathered these various storms?

4.4.2.1 In broad terms Buddhism, which has been in Japan for over 1400 years, is an important part of the country's cultural heritage. Its literature, painting, sculpture, and architecture continue to attract attention. Also, because it has moulded the Japanese mind for almost as long, Buddhism remains present, at a deep level, in an atavistic feeling of the fleeting nature of things, of the precariousness of the individual, and in a morality of detachment and self-control in the face of the vagaries of life.

4.4.2.2 When we ask to what extent Japanese Buddhists retain conscious and deliberate adherence to their religion, we find that the situation is varied and is conditioned by many factors: age is the most obvious—all the opinion polls show lack of knowledge about, and a weaker attachment to, their religion amongst younger people; sex is another—women are more devout than men. Education is a third factor of considerable importance—formerly the monasteries were the centres of general education which they dispensed together with religious instruction. It was common practice to enter them for educational purposes, for quite long periods of study. Today the official educational institutions are secular and seek to inculcate secularist attitudes. Their effect is to produce a 'lay' or 'scientific' mentality, inclined to reject the 'transrational'. Under this pressure many young intellectuals lose their religious belief. Those who are older or who, despite everything, cling on to their faith in order to justify themselves, seek to show that Buddhism is in accord with science in that it possesses scientific methods and is an answer to modern problems.

4.4.2.3 As education, either through the schools or the mass media, is extremely widespread in Japan, the conscious questioning of Buddhism and other religions in the light of scientific facts or theories is intense. F. M. Basabe,[1] a professor at the Sophia University of Tokyo, has made a very informative survey of about 1,600 men from sixty-nine urban centres in the Tokyo-Yokohama and Osaka-Kobe regions. The results show that in ___—or at least in these regions—the number of men who claim to belong ___finite religion is 14 per cent, or according to a slightly broader ___ 18 per cent; of these 'believers' 65.1 per cent are traditional ___d 34.9 per cent are adherents of Soka Gakkai (see §4.4.2.9 ___e who are indifferent to religion constitute 60 per cent of the ___non-believers 22.1 per cent. Among the latter, the age group ___ for more than the group 30–39. Also those who are ___ved are more likely to be non-believers than the well-to-do.

___ symptom, on the conscious level, of certain fundamental ___n man in a state of crisis. This accounts for the appeal of ___ns of faith to Buddhist family piety, and explains why ___ observance still draw crowds to sanctuaries, especially

___ *Attitudes of Japanese Men*, Tokyo.

those connected with the cult of Amida. Furthermore, the crushing of the individual by the great economic, industrial, urban and political monoliths of modern society has led, in some cases, to a kind of 'personalist' revolt which marks a return to individualism and to the interior, meditative quest of Zen. Thus some of the major traditional currents continue, and some of their spiritual centres attract even visitors from the West who are going through the same crisis and are engaged in the same quest.

4.4.2.5 Popular devotion is, however, still very evident, especially at the most famous temples and centres of pilgrimage. Although the following passage was written some fifty years ago, the description it gives of Buddhist devotion in Japanese temples and shrines is still applicable today, and scenes such as this can still be witnessed frequently:

> The worshipper on entering sounds this bell, or claps his hands and usually throws a coin into the coin receptacle, and there stands for some moments in prayer, making low bows or protestations at the end. Family parties appear, father, mother, and several children: they kneel, intone prayers, and pass out. An old woman has been sitting as near the altar as she can get for a long time, mumbling the Namu Amida and recording its repetitions on a rosary. A man is reading a Sutra to himself in an audible voice—in Nichiren temples sometimes accompanying the reading by gently sounding a wooden gong. Outside, a specially zealous devotee is apparently carrying out a vow by circumambulating the temple a great many times, repeating prayers as he goes. The impression one gets at a great city temple like the Asakusa in Tokyo, from the unceasing procession of worshippers, arriving, praying, and departing, is very considerable. Possibly more impressive is it to step into some smaller shrine and find it quite empty save for the merciful Amida and one lone worshipper, a woman, sobbing out her broken heart before him.
>
> (Pratt, J. B. (1928) *op. cit.*, p. 544)

4.4.2.6 A passage in the *Encyclopedia* (p. 341) summarizes concisely several major aspects of modern Buddhism in Japan and rightly emphasizes two influences to which Buddhism has been subjected: that is, the influence of Christianity both in the sense of presenting a more 'personalized' religion and in the sense of urging social service to other men; and the influence of secular scholarship on Buddhist studies. The latter has involved the critical study of sources and a new awareness of Buddhism as an historical cultural reality. Buddhism is now engaged in propaganda and missionary work not only in Japan but outside chiefly in the 'Western' world.

4.4.2.7 The most characteristic phenomenon of this impact of new ideologies and initiatives upon classical Buddhism has been the creation of certain 'New Religions', as they are called. This creation of 'sects' is of course part of the Japanese tradition, but there has been an enormous and unprecedented development since the last war. Within Buddhism alone, between 1945 and 1961 the number of officially recognized denominations increased from 28 to 260. The religious groups which came into the category of 'others' (i.e. not counting Shintōism, Buddhism and Christianity) rose to a total of 156. Of these independent sects some rejected any link with older religions whilst others, consciously or unconsciously, retained something from their heritage, notably certain Buddhist ideas.

4.4.2.8 An official Japanese government publication gives a picture of this situation in all its variety.[1]

| NAME OF MOVEMENT | NUMBER OF GROUPS | NUMBERS 1966 | NUMBERS 1972 |
|---|---|---|---|
| Tendai (philosophical) | 19 | 4,317,000 | 4,665,000 |
| Shingon (open) | 48 | 11,871,000 | 11,177,000 |
| Pure Land (devotional) | 25 | 17,541,000 | 20,941,000 |
| Zen (meditative) | 23 | 4,660,000 | 10,150,000 |
| Nichiren (proselytizing) | 37 | 27,419,000 | 31,887,000 |
| Others (diverse) | 8? | 1,400,000 | 2,500,000 |

Among those classified as 'others' (New Religions) many are of short duration.

4.4.2.9 From the above table it is clear that the two most representative tendencies—which are still growing—are those of devotion (Pure Land, Jōdo) and proselytism (Nichiren). Enough has already been said above about Jōdo, but some mention must be made here of the most militant of the contemporary movements, which still appeals to the name of its medieval founder Nichiren (1222–1283); see §3.2.3 above). His movement rejected all other tendencies—contemplative, devotional or ritualistic. It proclaimed instead a message of condemnation—of the perverse world in general, and in particular of a Japan which it considered to be in a state of decadence. The most famous and vigorous modern successor of the Nichiren movement is *Soka Gakkai*, which means 'value-creating academic-Society'. By 1970 it had a membership of more than 26,000,000 adherents. Read the account in *Ling*, §7.48, of the rise and great political importance of this sect.

4.4.2.10 Once again, you may ask whether there is not a contradiction between the militancy of sects such as Soka Gakkai and the non-violent ideals of Buddhism. But remember that there are different kinds of Buddhism and different kinds of Buddhists. With their anxiety, their fluctuation and their combative spirit, the New Religions 'are socio-religious movement of a Japan in transition. . . . They depict the struggle of a nation which is fighting for spiritual survival'.[2] These sects are seeking another meaning for life beyond material prosperity. With their programmes of involvement in social reform and even in politics, some Japanese Buddhists are returning, in a sense, to Asóka's old ideal of the 'moralization' of the State through the influence of Buddhist principles and communities, and their example of intransigent honesty. In the course of our discussion we have seen the benefits and the drawbacks of this age-old involvement of the Buddhist religion in civic society. For a fuller inquiry into the religious situation of Japan you will find it useful to consult the books[3] already cited.

---

[1] Agency for Cultural Affairs (1972) *Japanese Religion, A Survey by the Agency for Cultural Affairs*, Tokyo.

[2] Jaeckel, T. (1960) 'Psychological and Sociological Approaches to Japan's New Religions' in *Japanese Religions*, Vol. II, No. 1, p. 11.

[3] Basabe, F. M. (1968) *op. cit.*, pp. 116–121; Agency for Cultural Affairs (1972) *op. cit.*, pp. 66–69.

# 5    GENERAL CONCLUSIONS

## 5.1    A review of the unit

Having made an overall survey of Buddhism, of its history and of its situation in modern times it is obviously very difficult to provide a simple summing-up. However a few words, by way of conclusion, can be said concerning this 'religious quest' which has lasted for over 2500 years and has affected a large part of Asia.

Until the present day the mass of the Buddhist populations have remained attached to the mixture of essential Buddhism and elementary rituals which have always characterized their practice.

The Buddhist élites have been subjected to great changes: either from outside, as is the case with persecution in China or political and economic disestablishment in Japan, or from inside, stemming from the critical, secularist and materialist mentality of modern society. The élites have reacted in various ways to these immense changes, of which they are more aware than the masses.

In Buddhism, as in all religions, some laymen, and even monks, have become indifferent to, or have actually abandoned their religion. On the other hand the most steadfast have tried to react to the new situation in several ways: by reform of the monastic life, intended to lead to an increase in 'spirituality'; by greater activity in the outside world in the form of scholarly research, social work, and missionary activity outside Asia; by the regrouping of all the Sanghas, local, regional and national into stronger units, culminating in the World Federation of Buddhists and in the resumption of 'Councils' on a world scale held at intervals to discuss doctrine and action.

In some countries of Theravāda persuasion, Ceylon, Burma and Thailand, this revival is seen as a return to authenticity and to the spiritual unity of the population. On this account it enjoys the sympathy and even financial support of some governments and rulers.

Whereas Buddhism has been the victim of violent opposition or decadence in some of its traditional domains, it has found converts in the West and, as a result, for about a century it has benefitted from new financial, scholarly or religious support.

The Buddhist quest as we have attempted to describe it, both theoretically and historically, in all its variety, remains in our own day an *immense reality*.

## 5.2    The 'From what?'/'To what?'/'By what?' of Buddhism

Here, at the end of our description of Buddhism it will be in place for you to revise the whole material you have been studying by asking of Buddhism the three basic questions which provide the overall theme of our course:

(i)  *From* what does Buddhism provide liberation for man in his religious quest?

(ii)  *To* what does it lead him?

(iii)  *By* what means does it show him that he can make this progression?

Your answers would have to take account of the rich variety of religious traditions and interpretations within Buddhism; but it should not be difficult for you now to pick out the main features of this great world religion which provide the answers to our three questions. It will also be illuminating if you work through the thirteen subsidiary questions on our theme, given in Unit 1, §5 and consider their relevance to the Buddhist quest. I will not offer 'specimen answers' to this final revision exercise, but working out your own answers should be rewarding for you, by bringing into focus the variegated pattern of Buddhist religion that we have been studying.

(a)

*Figure 27 Wesak, London Buddhist Vihara, 1 May 1977: (a) Address; (b) Exterior of London Vihara; (c) Offerings; (d) Communal group.*

(b)

(c)

(d)

# 6 AN IMPRESSION OF ZEN BUDDHISM

*Written for the Course Team by Margaret Hall*

In recent years Zen Buddhism has attracted a good deal of attention in the West. This has perhaps been more the case in America than in Europe but nevertheless there seems to be sufficient general interest and curiosity about this particular spiritual phenomenon to warrant our giving a little more space to it in these units.

You will recall Professor Masson's treatment of Zen Buddhism in §§3.2.1. 13–3.2.1.14. What follows is meant to complement what was said there, and you will find it useful to refer back to those paragraphs before reading on.

*Figure 28  Detail of Hakuin's ink painting of Bodhidharma. (Private collection reproduced from* Zen Painting *by Yasuichi Awakawa, 1970 by courtesy of Kodansha International Publishing Ltd, Japan.)*

## 6.1 Legendary origins of Zen

> A special transmission outside the Scriptures;
> No dependence upon words and letters;
> Direct pointing to the heart of man;
> Seeing into one's nature and being a Buddha.

Thus runs the traditional four-phrase summary of Zen,[1] and it is this which is also expressed in its legendary history. Traditionally, Zen traces its origins back to the 'flower sermon' of the Buddha, which consisted of the Buddha's silently holding up a flower and smiling. The meaning of this 'sermon' was immediately, intuitively understood by the disciple, Mahākāśyapa, and this understanding was passed on, in the same way, until Bodhidharma, twenty-eighth in line from the Buddha, took it to China, where it flourished. You can read something of its history in China in the *Encyclopedia*, pages 331–333.

## 6.2 Zen and Tao

Once a great tradition has been established, it is all but impossible to tease out the various strands which have gone to its making, but it seems that Zen, as it is known in Japan today, originated in China as the result of an assimilation of certain Mahāyāna Buddhist ideas and Chinese ideas about the Tao—the great Way. (See §3.2.1.12 above). There is more detailed treatment of Taoism in the article by Werner Eichhorn (*Encyclopedia*, pp. 374–392). The sections on pages 375–377 of the article 'The School of Lao-tzŭ and Chuang-tzŭ', 'Tao, "The Way"' and 'Te, or "Virtue"' are particularly relevant to our discussion. Here are some lines from the *Tao te Ching*:

> The Tao that can be expressed is not the eternal Tao;
> The name that can be named is not the eternal name.
> Nameless, it is the origin of Heaven and Earth;
> Namable, it is the mother of all things.
>
> He who knows does not speak.
> He who speaks does not know.
>
> You look at it, but it is not to be seen;
> Its name is Formless.
>
> You listen to it, but it is not to be heard;
> Its name is soundless.
> You grasp it, but it is not to be held;
> Its name is Bodiless.
> These three elude all scrutiny,
> And hence they blend and become one.
>
> It is called formless form, thingless image;
> It is called the elusive, the evasive.
> Confronting it, you do not see its face;
> Following it, you do not see its back.

[1] 'Zen' is a Japanized form of the Chinese word 'Ch'an' from Sanskrit *dhyana* (meditation). Where the word means the Zen sect or school of Buddhism, I have used a capital Z. Where it means 'meditation' I have spelt it with a small z.

If you compared these with the Zen sayings in *Reader*, §3.5.6 'Japanese Sources' you will surely be struck by the similarities: the same delight in paradox; similar ideas, almost the same words are used by Daitō Kokushi to express The Ultimate Reality.

Another important Taoist element which one finds also in Zen is an emphasis on naturalness and spontaneity which comes of what is called in Chinese '*wu-wei*' (see §3.2.1.12 above). This is a difficult term to translate, but perhaps the least misleading English words are 'non-assertion' or 'non-striving', in the sense of not asserting the ego, but losing it and thus being in harmony with one's true nature and the nature of the universe, which is in fact one and the same Tao. The idea is that most of our action in the world is not harmonious, because it is centred in and springs from the ego, the little 'I' which, in our ignorance, we mistake for our true selves. If we can transcend this and realize our identity with the great Tao only then do we become capable of truly harmonious action, which does not conflict with our own natures, with others, or with the great Nature which contains all living things.

## 6.3  Zen and Art

The knowledge of this Tao is one which transcends the merely intellectual or anything that can be expressed in words. It is a knowledge which can best be expressed in action and in art. These ideas have had far-reaching implications for the culture of the Far East. This is a vast and fascinating subject which you can follow up in such books as *Zen Buddhism and Its Relation to Art*,[1] and *Zen Buddhism and its Influence on Japanese Culture*.[2]

*Figure 29   Ensō by Tōrei (Private collection reproduced by Yasuichi Awakawa, 1970 by courtesy of Kodansha International Publishing Ltd. Japan.)*

[1] Waley, A. (1922) *Zen Buddhism and its Relation to Art*, Luzac, London.
[2] Suzuki, D. T. (1938) *Zen Buddhism and its Influence on Japanese Culture*, Eastern Buddhist Society, Kyōto.

In this unit we have included four examples of *zenga* (literally 'Zen picture', in Japanese), and by looking at these illustrations you can probably get some feeling of how the Zen experience expresses itself in art. Zen masters are almost always highly accomplished calligraphers; in China and Japan calligraphy is a very ancient art form, allied to *sumi-e* (Japanese: drawings in black Chinese ink.) Sumi-e are favoured by Zen artists because of the extreme simplicity of the monochrome, together with the possibility it affords of infinite subtleties of shading. Zen always avoids loud colours or ostentation of any sort. Indeed there is a saying that, to the enlightened eye, the richest colours are contained in the black ink on the white paper.

*Figure 30 'Mu'. This is an example of a contemporary zenga. (Private collection reproduced from Zen Painting by Yasuichi Awakawa, 1970, by courtesy of Kodansha International Publishing Ltd., Japan.)*

To draw well in this medium requires absolute sureness of touch. The brush is made of bamboo, tipped with very soft hair, and the paper absorbs the ink immediately. Since every stroke counts, there is no room for any false stroke. In the hand of a skilled artist, however, a few strokes are enough, and it can be done in a few seconds. The control must be perfect, and spontaneous; in other words it is not a matter of following a set of external rules, but of obeying ones own 'True nature' which once one has discovered it cannot but result in exactly the right stroke or action. This has its parallel in all the Japanese arts, including the martial arts like *kendō* (the way of the sword) and *karate* (empty hand). The perfect karate chop can be no less an expression of Zen than the brush-stroke of the master calligrapher!

Three of the zenga in this unit are all of well-known Zen subjects: Bodhidharma, the legendary first patriarch (in this case by Hakuin, a great eighteenth century Japanese Zen master); an example of an *ensō* the symbolic expression of enlightenment; and the Chinese character *wu* (Japanese: *mu*) 'nothing', or 'void'. Besides relating to a centrally important concept of Mahāyāna Buddhism, this character also refers to the 'mu' kōan, which is one of the kōan which Zen practitioners may be given to meditate on. The anecdote which gave rise to the kōan is given on page 333 of the *Encylopedia*: Chao-chou (a master of the T'ang dynasty) was asked by a monk whether a dog possesses Buddha-nature. The reply was 'wu'. The question is what does this 'wu' really mean? It is more ambiguous than the English translation 'No' suggests.

## 6.4   Zen practice

Talking about kōan leads naturally on to the consideration of what is, when all is said and done, the central issue in Zen, the practice which aims to lead to enlightenment, for this is what the Zen quest is all about. First I want to say something about the 'setting' of this practice.

### 6.4.1   The temple

The Zen temple is quite small (even the large temples, such as Daitokuji, in Kyōto, actually consist of a complex of small temples, each in its own grounds). The feeling is one of intimacy and a kind of rustic simplicity, quite unlike that of the Shingon temples, with their images, mandala and wafting incense. The screens open out on to the landscaped garden; it may be a 'rock and sand' garden of the unique Zen kind, for the disposition of sand and rocks in a particular design is another means of artistic expression of Zen. The rooms flexibly divide off from one another by means of wood and paper screens. They are, in fact, no different from those in an ordinary Japanese house, except that one will contain an altar and *mokugyō* ('wooden fish'), a kind of wooden drum, said to resemble a fish, which is struck as an accompaniment to sūtra-chanting

6.4.1.1 The central building however is the *zendō* or meditation hall where *zazen* takes place. In the Rinzai sect this has two raised platforms, running down each side of the room, on which the practitioners sit, facing each other. In the Sōtō sect, they sit facing the wall. In fact this doesn't make much difference, sinze in zazen the eyes are cast down anyway.

6.4.1.2 The zendō is used by the monks every day, for several hours, and many temples also hold special sessions for lay people. It is quite common in Japan, for both men and women, to have done what they call 'Zen training' at some time in their lives, usually in their youth. This kind of zen, technically called *bompu* (ordinary), has a function akin to the kind of hatha yoga which is popular in this country at present.

### 6.4.2   The five kinds of Zen

6.4.2.1 From the point of view of Zen Buddhism, there are five kinds of zen, or meditation, in an ascending scale, the lowest, or shallowest, of which is *bompu*. Next comes *gedō*, which means 'outside way' in Japanese. This covers the kinds of meditation or contemplation practised in religions other than Buddhism, such as Hindu yoga or Christian contemplation. The point that Zen Buddhists make about gedō is that these kinds of meditation practices are often done, not with the aim of achieving the supreme enlightenment, but of cultivating super-human powers, such as the ability to walk unhurt on broken glass, to heal illnesses and so on. Zen Buddhists do not deny that the assiduous practice of meditation may result in these miraculous abilities but they are not the end, and the worst that can happen is that a person should be so beguiled by them as to cultivate them for their own sake and lose sight of the ultimate aim.

6.4.2.2 The next kind of meditation is that of *shōjō* (Japanese for 'small vehicle' or 'Hīnayāna.) From the point of view of Zen Buddhism, being a branch of the Mahāyāna tradition, this kind of meditation is truly Buddhist but not in accord with the Buddha's highest teaching. The reason for this is that meditation in the shōjō tradition is concerned only with the salvation of that particular individual, and does not go further to the idea of attaining salvation 'for the weal of the world'. From a Zen point of view also, the Hīnayāna vision of life seems somewhat bleak and negative. In Zen the enlightened mind is definitely life-affirming.

6.4.2.3 The fourth classification is the Mahāyāna kind (*daijō*—great vehicle in Japanese), and the essence of this is 'seeing into your esssential nature and realizing the Way in your daily life.' To this end, various techniques of meditation have been evolved; in the Rinzai, the kōan method has been systematized.

6.4.2.4 The fifth and highest form is called *saijōjō*. Strictly speaking this is not really distinguishable from daijō. It is a form of daijō which is given particulr emphasis in the Sōtō sect. It is characterized by the form of zazen known as *shikan-taza*, which means 'just sitting'; just sitting as opposed to concentrating on one's breathing or one's kōan, for example. Since there is no object of concentration, this is the purest form of concentration possible. It is also the most difficult, that is, for the mind which has not broken through to the state where subject and object no longer exist. It is the expression of the Buddha-mind. This is how the Buddha is seen sitting in the thousands of images of him, all over Japan. It is a state of perfect equilibrium and serenity. In the Rinzai sect it is most commonly practised by those who are far advanced along the path.

### 6.4.3 Zazen

Finally I want to talk about zazen itself, and to show how it is the centre of an integrated system, every part of which is directed towards the one end of attaining the supreme realisation.

The actual sitting posture itself, which ideally should be the lotus position ie: with neck and back straight, legs crossed and feet resting, soles upwards, upon the thighs, is said to be the one most conducive to equilibrium of body and mind. Only those with long experience, however, can sustain this position for hours at a time; novices and lay people, at least, are not expected to do so. At a typical *sesshin* for lay people for example, the day is varied in a number of ways. Such a sesshin is a kind of concentrated Zen life over a short period, a day, a weekend or a week, and includes most of the elements of monastic Zen life, apart from begging.

The day starts, at around 4 am, with sūtra-chanting. Apart from expressing reverence to the Buddha and the great teachings of Buddhism, sūtra-chanting is considered, in Zen, as a mode of zazen, ie: as a way of concentrating the mind, of freeing it from discursive thought. Then follows a period of zazen proper, before breakfast which, like the mid-day and evening meals[1], is a simple meal of rice and vegetables, taken in absolute silence. The way of taking a Zen meal is to sustain quietness of mind and freedom from discursive thought by concentrating completely on what one is doing, no matter how trivial, such as taking up chopsticks or the taste of the food itself. This attitude of total 'mindfulness' pervades the whole day, and when everything is undertaken in this spirit, it can rightly be said that everything one does becomes a mode of zazen. The effect of such a discipline is to develop the powers of sense-awareness enormously. Hence the great sensitivity one finds in Zen towards Nature, and the expression of appreciation of natural beauty in painting, poetry and landscape gardening.

At some time in the morning there will be a period of manual work, which usually takes the form of cleaning the temple or tidying the garden. Needless to say, this is also done with the kind of 'mindfulness' I have been talking about. It is an expression of the Zen concern with the practical and the ordinary, everyday life of the world.

Also in the morning, the master gives his sermon. You will find a good example of a sermon of this kind in the *Reader*, §3.8. It is the 'Sermon on One mind', by the fourteenth century Japanese Master, Bassui. Besides the general sermon, each student has a formal interview or *dokusan* with the Master, towards the end of sesshin. In this he may be questioned about his kōan or discuss any specific problems which have arisen during zazen. A skilled master has an intuitive understanding of the stage a student has reached and, like a good teacher, adapts his response accordingly. He can be kind, and encouraging, or (unlike a good teacher perhaps!) abrupt, even violent, if he feels that will help the student to the final goal (see above, §3.2.1.14(d) and (e) and the references given there).

## 6.5 The ten ox-herding pictures

Fortunately, the stages of the Zen quest are set out very clearly, in this famous series of drawings and commentaries, which you will find in the *Reader*, §3.9. The original drawings (not those reproduced in the *Reader*) and the commentaries are attributed to Kuo-an Shih-yuan, a Chinese Zen Master ᶜ the twelfth century. Actually his are the earliest surviving ones, although it ⸮nown there were earlier versions now lost. The ox has always been ⸮red in India, and allusions to it are frequent in the scriptures of both ⸮yāna and Mahāyāna Buddhism.

Exercise

⸮t that you read Bassui's sermon (*Reader*, §3.8), look at the Ten ⸮ng pictures with the commentaries (*Reader*, §3.9), and test your own ⸮nding of them by writing out an interpretation of each.

[1] It is l⸮
noon. In⸮n in the vinaya rules that only one main meal a day must be taken, and no food after
evening, b⸮lder, northern countries however, it was found essential for health to take food in the
⸮s food is still not regarded as a proper meal but as 'medicine'.

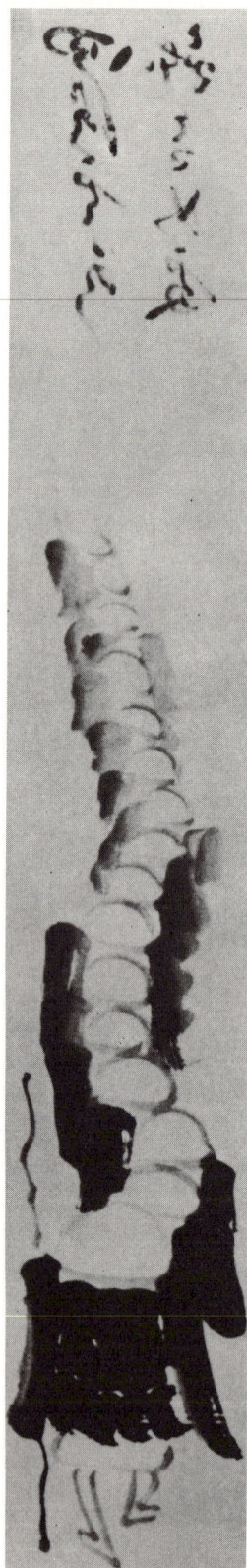

*110*

Figure 31 Nantembō. Novices going to beg. (Private collection reproduced from Zen Painting by Yasuichi Awakawa, 1970 by courtesy of Kodansha International Publishing Ltd, Japan.) In this picture the artist shows Zen novices setting out to seek alms at houses in the neighbourhood. Such humble tasks, he indicates, are the very essence of Zen religious practice.

## 6.5.2 Specimen answer and discussion

(i) The very first two lines express the idea that one's True nature is the Buddha nature, if one could but realize it. From the point of view of this realization it is obviously absurd to seek for something which has never really got lost. But the man is not in a state of realization. His state is one of alienation, anxiety and moral confusion; to use the Buddhist term, of illusion, or ignorance. The delusions of the senses means something more fundamental than pursuing sensual pleasures. It means being taken in by appearances i.e.: the appearance that 'I' am separate and distinct from 'the other' i.e.: the objects of my senses. It is this fundamental illusion which gives rise to desire or 'grasping' after those objects, and to fear of losing them, once possessed. The irony is, that at this stage, enlightenment itself is seen as something outside oneself to be possessed or achieved; hence the illusion of 'searching' for one's True-nature.

(ii) The stage described here is that of merely intellectual understanding, which has come about through study of the sūtras and teachings. A perfect elucidation of the distinction between this intellectual understanding and actual experience is to be found in the story of Hui-neng (the sixth patriarch of Zen in China) and Shen-hsiu which you can read on page 332 of the *Encyclopedia*.

(iii) In this stage the breakthrough occurs: the seeker experiences 'satori', and his attitude to life is revolutionized. The same sense-experience which was previously a source of delusion is now seen as 'no different from the true Source', which is, in turn, 'no different' from his 'True-nature'. Such an experience nullifies 'grasping' since he experiences the universe as himself, and desire can only arise in a situation of 'I' and 'not I'.

(iv) This experience of 'satori' is however only the beginning. It is all too easy to slip back into the old state of mind. At this stage conscious effort and self-discipline is required.

(v) Just as enlightenment gives validity to sense experience, it gives validity to discursive thought also. The state of mind is paramount; therefore discipline of the mind is essential.

(vi) Finally a stage is reached where there is no further danger of slipping back. As before, the 'gain' and 'loss' mentioned here refer to the anxiety about achieving enlightenment, as well as the everyday anxieties about life in the world. The state of mind now is characterized by tranquillity and lightheartedness.

(vii) Now that the seeker is in a state completely transcending all duality, the symbol of the ox has served its purpose. Now he knows that there never was an 'ox' to be caught. The image of the net and the fish, incidentally, is from Chuang Tzŭ, the great Taoist philosopher.

(viii) Neither was there a 'self' to be realized. This stage represents the ultimate state of realization, symbolized in the ink-painting by a perfect circle, drawn with one stroke of the brush. This circle is the symbol of the 'void', and we can say now that the self is 'void': a condition of absolute purity, in which even the apparent opposites of worldliness and holiness, of enlightenment and non-enlightenment, Buddahood and non-Buddhahood, have disappeared. Since the man does not show any of these recognizable qualities, 'even one with a thousand eyes cannot discern what he is'. The idea is repeated later on, in the tenth stage; 'even the wisest do not know him' and 'his mind is hidden'. It is expressed again, here, in the reference to the story of Hoyu-zenji, a Zen master of the T'ang dynasty who had such an aura of holiness that the birds brought him flowers. When he became fully enlightened, however, the birds ceased their offerings, because he no longer gave off any aura of holiness.

(ix) Now that he has realized the purity which has, in reality, always been his, the man who has reached enlightenment lives a life of complete naturalness and spontaneity. There is no further need for the artificial effort required at an earlier stage; sitting (za-zen), for instance, will no longer be an act of self-discipline, but a natural expression of the Buddha-nature. The state of flux in the world no longer bothers him, because he no longer has the illusion of himself as something static or permanent outside of it. 'The waters are blue, the mountains are green', a sentence of consummate poetry, expresses the essence of his experience. In a sense nothing has changed, yet how much has changed! To the enlightened mind, the simple joy in sense experience has a new sufficiency. Perhaps you noticed the Taoist flavour of this whole passage.

(x) He lives a perfectly ordinary life in the world, symbolized by the market or the city (which is the same word in Chinese). He drinks wine—his gourd is for carrying it, and presumably eats fish—neither of which a Buddhist monk would do. But—and here is the typically Mahāyāna emphasis—his hands are bliss-bestowing; he is the means of enlightenment to others in the world.

# 7 FURTHER READING

## 7.1 Dictionaries

Humphreys, C. (1976) *A Popular Dictionary of Buddhism*, (2nd ed) Curzon Press, London.

Nakamura, H., *et al.* (1965) *Japanese-English Buddhist Dictionary*, Daito Shuppansha, Tokyo.

Nyanatiloka, Bhikku (1956) *Buddhist Dictionary: Manual of Buddhist Terms*, Frewin, Colombo.

Rhys-Davids, T. W. and Stede, W. (1972) *Pali-English Dictionary*, Pali Text Society.

## 7.2 Texts (in translation)

Burtt, E. A. (1955) *The Teachings of the Compassionate Buddha*, Mentor/New American Library, New York.

Müller, M. (ed) (1900) *The Sacred Books of the East*, Oxford University Press.

Müller, M. and Rhys-Davids, T. W. (eds) (1895–1910) *The Sacred Books of the Buddhists*, Luzac, London.

All relevant editions published by *The Pali Text Society*, London.

Conze, E., *et al.* (1954), *Buddhist Texts through the Ages*, Oxford, Bruno Cassirer.

Goddard, D. (1970) *A Buddhist Bible*, Beacon Press, Boston.

Humphreys, C. (1970) *The Wisdom of Buddhism*, Rider, London.

Warren, H. C. (1909) *Buddhism in Translations*, Harvard University Press.

## 7.3 General studies

Conze, E. (1959) *Buddhism, its Essence and Development*, Bruno Cassirer, Oxford.

Humphreys, C. (1951) *Buddhism*, Penguin, Harmondsworth.

Kern, H. (1896) *Manual of Indian Buddhism*, K. J. Trubner, Strasburg.

Masson, J. (1975) *Le bouddhisme, chemin de libération*, Desclée de Brouwer, Paris.

Masson, J. (1942) *Le religion populaire dans le canon pali*, Bibliothêque du Muséon, Louvain.

Suzuki, B. L. (1969) *Mahayana Buddhism*, Allen & Unwin, London.

## 7.4 Buddha and the origins of Buddhism

Brewster, E. H. (1962) *The life of Gotama the Buddha*, Routledge Kegan Paul, London.

Lamotte, E. (1958) *Histoire du Bouddhisme Indien*, Bibliothêque du Muséon, Louvain.

Nanamoli Thera (1972) *The life of Buddha* (according to Pali Texts), Kandy.

Oldenberg, H. (1882) *The Buddha, His Life, His Doctrine, His Community*, Williams & Norgate, London.

Thomas, E. J. (1927) *The Life of Buddha as Legend and History*, Routledge Kegan Paul, London.

## 7.5  Dhamma

Conze, E. (1962) *Buddhist Thought in India*, Allen & Unwin, London.

Morgan, K. W. (1956) *The Path of The Buddha, Buddhism interpreted by Buddhists*, Ronald Press Company, New York.

Murti, T. R. V. (1955) *The Central Philosophy of Buddhism*, Allen & Unwin, London.

Rahula, W. (1959) *What the Buddha taught*, G. Fraser, Bedford.

Stcherbatski, F. I. (1965) (reprint) *The Conception of Buddhist Nirvāna*, Mouton, Hague.

Takakusu, J. (1973) *The Essentials of Buddhist Philosophy*, Greenwood Press.

Takibana, S. (1961) *The Ethics of Buddhism*, Colombo.

Thomas, E. J. (1951) *History of Buddhist Thought*, Routledge Kegan Paul, London.


## 7.6  Sangha

Conze, E. (1972) *Buddhist Meditation*, (2nd ed). Allen & Unwin. London.

Dutt, S. (1963) *Buddhist Monks and Monasteries in India*, Allen & Unwin, London.

Dutt, S. (1960) *Early Monastic Buddhism*, Asian Publishing House, Calcutta.


## 7.7  Buddhism in Sri Lanka

Houtart, F. (1974) *Religion and Ideology in Sri Lanka*, Hansa Publications, Colombo.

Pratt, J. B. (1928) *The Pilgrimage of Buddhism*, Macmillan, London.

De Silva, L. A. (1974) *Buddhism, Beliefs and Practices in Sri Lanka*, Christian Study Centre Division of Buddhist Studies, Columbo.


## 7.8  Buddhism in China

Pratt, J. B. (1928) *The Pilgrimage of Buddhism*, Macmillan, London.

Welch, H. (1967) *The Practice of Chinese Buddhism 1900–1950*, Harvard University Press.

Welch, H. (1968) *The Buddhist Revival in China*, Harvard University Press.

Welch, H. (1972) *Buddhism under Mao*, Harvard University Press.


## 7.9  Buddhism in Japan

Anesaki, M. (1963) *History of Japanese Religion*, Tuttle, Rutland (Vermont).

Brannen, N. S. (1965) *Soka Gakkai: Japan's Militant Buddhists*, John Knox Press, Richmond.

Earhart, H. D. (1970) *The New Religions of Japan*, Sophia University Press, Tokyo.

Hammer, R. (1962) *Japan's Religious Ferment*, Oxford University Press.

Murata, K. (1969) *Japan's New Buddhism: An Objective Account of Soka Gakkai*, Walker/Weatherhill, New York.

Pratt, J. B. (1928) *op. cit.*, Chapters XXII–XXXI.

Spae, J. (1971) *Japanese Religiosity*, Oriens Institute for Religious Research, Tokyo.

Suzuki, D. T. (1974) *Manual of Zen Buddhism*, Rider, London.

Suzuki, D. T. (1938) *Zen Buddhism and its Influence on Japanese Culture*, Eastern Buddhist Society, Kyoto (reprinted in the Bollingen Series).

Van Straelen, H. and Offner, C. B. (1963) *Modern Japanese Religions*, E. J. Brill, London.

Waley A. (1922) *Zen Buddhism and its Relation to Art*, Luzac, London.

Watts, A. W. (1962) *The Way of Zen*, Penguin, Harmondsworth.

## ACKNOWLEDGEMENT

Grateful acknowledgement is made to Mrs Catherine M. Pratt for permission to reprint extracts from J. B. Pratt, *The Pilgrimage of Buddhism*, Macmillan Publishing Co. Inc, New York, 1928.